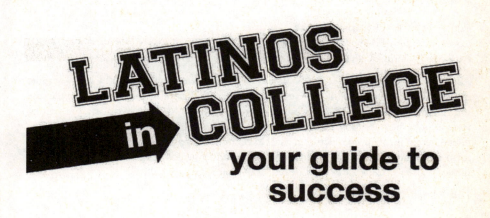

LATINOS in COLLEGE

your guide to success

Mariela Dabbah

First Edition: 2009

Published by: Consultare

208 Kemeys Avenue
Scarborough, NY 10510
www.latinosincollege.com

This publication is designed to provide accurate and authoritative information regarding the subject matter covered. It is sold with the understanding that the publisher is not engaged in rendering legal, accounting or other professional service. If legal advice or other expert assistant is required, the services of a competent professional should be sought.

From a Declaration of Principles Jointly Adopted by a Committee of the American Bar Association and a Committee of Publishers and Associates

This book is not a substitute for legal, financial or tax advice.

Disclaimer required by Texas statutes.

ISBN: 978-0-615-23371-0

Printed and bound in the United States of America

To Cristina Alfaro,
for your friendship and your incredible
support and vision.

Latino families nationwide benefit from
your commitment to education.

ACKNOWLEDGMENTS

No book of mine is ever written without the contributions of many, many people. And being that this book is part of a national education campaign there are that many more people involved in its success than usual.

I wish to thank the following individuals for sharing their experiences with me and for participating in a long interview:

Jocelyn Acosta, Leylha Ahuile, Nara Alvarez, Teri Arvesu, Daisy Auger-Domínguez, Brian Campos, Luz Canino-Baker, Diana Baez, Gladys Bernett, John Cavallo, Jesús José Chávez, Martín Curiel, Yiné de la Cruz, José R. de la Torre, Rosanna Durruthy, Ana Esquivel, Alberto Ferreras, Dolores M. Fernández, Ph.D., Antonio R. Flores, Ph.D., Joseph E. García, Karina Hamman, Greg Hallman Jr., Rita Izaguirre, James Kopelman, Margaret Lazo, Henry Lescaille, Maira Mercado, Cathy Makunga, Louis Maldonado, Stacey Martínez, Wilson Martínez del Río, María Cecilia Mosquera, María Naranjo, Miguel R.Olivas-Luján, Patricia Pacheco, Mina Pacheco Nazemi, David Peña, Sylvia Pertzborn, Cristina Pinzón, Arturo Poiré, Jennifer Quijano, Carla Rivera, Marisela Riveros, Raquel Roque, Loida Rosario, Andrea Sáenz, Samuel Ulloa, Marcia Vargas, Paloma I. Veloz, Michael McKenzie, Lulú Wang.

To Ricardo Anzaldúa, for sharing his great story with me and in doing so, inspiring many Latinos with it.

Special thanks to Carla Rivera, my former intern, whose key insights I share throughout the book.

To Marjorie Venegas, thanks for reviewing the manuscript and offering your invaluable feedback.

To my incredible and unrelenting cheerleading squad, my friends who are always there no matter what it is I need to discuss or what time it is of day or night! Susan Landon, Marisol González, Arturo Poiré, Alex Michell and Gustavo Averbuj.

To Andrea Montejo, your guidance, encouragement and passion for my work are such a blessing.

To my friend Leylha Ahuile, you make everything easy for those around you and I'm no exception. Thanks for helping me jump through the hurdles.

Thanks to Chuck Hurewitz for keeping my best interests at heart.

To Luis Laviena, Gladys Bernett and Gloria Puentes I'm grateful for your enthusiasm and support.

My thanks to Gisela García, Frederick Martínez (el Pachá), Tucupay, Domingo and René, the team at WADO 1280 (Univisión Radio) who so openly welcomed me into their family.

To the members of the Advisory Council Board of my education campaign: "Latinos in College", my heartfelt thanks for your ideas, your time, your love for our students and your concern for their future.

Finally, to Renzo Martorella and Paul García, the latest additions to my team, thanks for becoming involved with this project.

CONTENTS

A FEW WORDS
BEFORE WE BEGIN

The last couple of years have been magical for me. Having the opportunity to work and speak to a wide range of audiences about the importance of education has been an incredible learning experience. Given the fact that I write, speak and consult on topics that help Latinos navigate the American system, I get to hear stories from high school students who received large scholarships and from their parents who are unaware of what they can do to help their kids make it to college; I hear from college students who want to know how to best prepare for life after school and from Latinos who work in corporate America and who wish to learn how to advance beyond middle management.

Above and beyond my own research and personal experience with the subject, my books are possible thanks to the individual stories that people tell me. In my quest to gather the pieces of the puzzle that will make Latino students' path to success a smooth one, I've tried to capture different angles of the Latino college experience through the stories of dozens of people.

So, if you are the first one in your family to attend college, read Chapter 2 where you will find insights and tools to deal with that situation. If you are a high school senior trying to decide on what school is best for you, Chapter 4 will guide you through the process. If you haven't considered studying abroad while in college, Chapter 15 will be a great eye opener.

I'm sure you'll find things in this book that you will identify with and others with which you won't. Take what you need for your journey and leave the rest behind so you travel light.

I wish you strength and the gift of persevere in your path to a college degree!

Saludos,
Mariela

INTRODUCTION

Congratulations! If you are reading this book it is because you are either going to college or are already in college, which means you already took several steps towards your success:

- You are doing or already did well in high school.

- You are graduating or have already graduated high school.

- You are learning to navigate or have already learned how to navigate the college application and financial aid processes.

- You are planning to overcome or have already overcome several barriers (cultural and otherwise) in order to enter college. You might even be the first in your family to attend.

Now that you made it to this level, don't expect to hear the familiar "lay back, relax and enjoy the show" message you hear at the movies after all the warnings about not smoking and turning off your cell phone. While deciding to go to college—or getting into one—is a very big deal, it is an even bigger deal to succeed at it. And no matter how much fun and fulfilling the experience can be, it also requires a whole lot of work. As a matter of fact, for the next few years, you will accumulate valuable experiences and form long-lasting bonds, but your main focus needs to be to GRADUATE from college and that is exactly what I hope this book will help you accomplish.

If you are already in college or if you're well on your way, you may be asking yourself: "Why would I need a college guide that is specifically for Latino students?" Yes, there are countless college guides out there and most of them cater to the general audience. After all, if we are all in college, what's the difference? Well, read on and you'll find out how your upbringing and your background affect your college experience.

And as you will see, this is exactly the reason why I decided to write a guide specifically for Latino students on this issue.

A few years ago, I started focusing my work and my writing on helping Latinos crack the American code, which means, helping them understand how the system works so that they can succeed in their education, job search, career, etc. As a Latino immigrant myself, I found that there was very little information available in this area. For instance, when I first arrived in this country, I had a hard time looking for a job because the job search process in the U.S. is vastly different from the one in Argentina.

As you might already know, Latino students have the highest high school dropout rate of any group (50 percent) one of the lowest college enrollment rates (20 percent) and one of the highest college dropout rates as well: only 12 out of 100 students who enroll in a 4-year college ultimately graduate, and only 14 percent make it to the third year[1]. Now you might be saying to yourself, "Well, those are just statistics, that's not me." And while I commend you for thinking this way, I also want

---

[1] Source: Pew Hispanic Center Mid Decade Report.

to ask you to think again. College can be a very confusing and difficult time to get through, and none of us are immune to the challenges that can arise from not knowing how to navigate the system. That is why, through this book I not only want us to radically change these statistics, I want to help you blossom through your college experience and succeed beyond your wildest dreams.

Studies show that over a lifetime people with a 4-year college degree make between $1 and $2 million more than people without a degree, and if that is not a compelling enough reason to study hard and graduate college, I don't know what is. Yet another very strong reason to add years to your education is that study after study in the U.S. and abroad, has shown a correlation between education level and longevity. Yes, the more you study, the longer you live! Although the reasons for this correlation are not completely clear, it is a well-established fact. Studying keeps you motivated and interested in life, and in my opinion, that is one of the best ways to live—always feeling curious about one's surroundings.

Statistics also show that college graduates have a lower level of joblessness than people without a college degree. So as you see, a college degree will not only help you get through bad economic times, it will give you a longer life and will contribute enormously to your future success, and probably contribute to your becoming a leader in the community. Having that coveted degree will open doors for you at every level in the corporate world, the public service sector and even if you decide to open your own business. The odds of succeeding at anything you wish to do will definitely be stacked in your favor.

Now, I don't want you to just graduate from college with a high GPA. No, I also want you to become a role model for those who come behind you, whether they are your younger siblings, your cousins or people you don't know. It is only by passing on our knowledge and experience that the Latino community will continue to get stronger and will realize its full potential. And as members of this community, we all have the responsibility to share our experience with others around us.

So, as I wish you the best of luck in this journey, I also hope you accept the challenge to pass on the baton! It will not only be your way of staying connected with your community, it will also be a way of giving back to all those who supported you through this crucial period of your life.

Chapter 1

A GOOD DOSE OF INSPIRATION TO GET YOU STARTED

Do you know what percentage of the U.S. population makes over $1 million a year? Less than 1 percent. Do you know how many Latinos fall into this category? Less than 0.5 percent! So the question is, what does it take to be so successful? Have these people always known what they wanted out of life? Did they have a clear career path from the very beginning?

Well, many of them did, but not all of them. Let me introduce you to Ricardo Anzaldúa, one of the members of this very selected group of earners. His journey has been full of twists and turns and, although it took him a while to figure out where he wanted to be, he persisted in his search until he found his passion.

Born in New Mexico to a Mexican father who didn't finish high school and a second generation Hispanic mother who did, Ricardo spent his youth living in Pharr, a Texan border town, where he went to school and worked.

Trying to find good jobs during his high school years wasn't easy. In the eyes of prospective employers, back in the late sixties, his Hispanic background limited him to working in the fields. One of the most memorable jobs he had was as a "flagman", the guy who indicates to aerial "crop dusters" where they needed to start their next pass so their pesticide applications wouldn't miss any part of the crop. "It was bad in the sense that I frequently got sprayed with pesticide", Ricardo says, "but it paid better than other agricultural jobs, so I was lucky to have it."

It was hard work but the time spent in the fields only made it clearer to him that the only way to move ahead was to graduate from high school (which he did, top of his class) and go to college in order to obtain a professional degree. This idea, however, would prove to be more elusive than he could have imagined, in part due to the fact that nobody in his entire family had ever gone to college. Ricardo had no frame of reference to help him or his parents understand what college entailed, what steps needed to be taken in order to get there and once there, what it would be like. It was an abstract idea. "Nobody in my family had gone to college, so nobody could tell me concretely that if I wanted to be a lawyer, I would need four years of college plus three years of law school," shares Ricardo.

And while Ricardo was ultimately able to reach the goals he had set out for himself, this lack of guidance had a long lasting effect on Ricardo's educational career. At many stages he lacked focus in what he was doing, and he ended up taking several detours that he may have been able to avoid, had he found someone to guide him, or a mentor along the way.

Ricardo began his college years at the Air Force Academy in Colorado Springs, CO. He was admitted at this very selective school at the recommendation of a Texas congressman from his town. "I think it's the same situation for the majority of applicants to military academies. You just send a letter to the congressman requesting the recommendation and he sends you a form," explains Ricardo. His intention was to be an Air Force lawyer and to fly planes (rather than being sprayed by them!). He only lasted three months, however, because he soon realized that the Academy was more interested in preparing officers than in providing a well-rounded education, the way more traditional college are. Most students came from military families and were interested in a military career, something that Ricardo wasn't looking for.

He returned to Texas and enrolled at the Pan American University (today, the University of Texas Pan American in Edinburg, Texas) while he began to send applications to top universities such as Harvard, Princeton and Stanford. But because he had started his studies somewhere else, these schools were seeing him as a transfer student, which complicated matters beyond what Ricardo felt he could handle at the time. So at seventeen, a little lost about his future and with nobody to guide him, he decided to move to San Francisco to live with an aunt. He found a job at a chip factory in Silicon Valley where he connected with a group of students from Brown University that were taking a year off. "I learned that at Brown you could design your own study program and as a matter of fact, I changed mine several times," explains Ricardo. He applied to Brown and as he was accepted, he moved to Providence, Rhode Island in 1974.

Interested in the world of ideas, Ricardo wanted to study philosophy and perhaps work at the university as a professor. Just as when he was younger, he was still very interested in learning, but had very little direction on what it took to build an academic career that would lead to a successful professional career later.

His professors encouraged him to be a professor. Ricardo feels that perhaps, they weren't aware of how education had changed since they had entered the profession and so, in turn, they weren't able to provide complete or insightful career advice.

"As time went by I not only realized that the time commitment to become a philosopher was extremely long (it took approximately eight years after college to obtain a Ph.D.), but also that philosophers spoke in a cryptic and technical lingo aimed at a small audience. I was more interested in impacting a larger audience," says Ricardo. His interest shifted to economics and economic development (particularly, the economic development of Latin American countries), an area that offered the application of ideas that would affect a much wider audience.

He graduated from Brown University in 1978 with a major in Latin American studies and a focus on Economic Development. The following year, Ricardo became the first Special Assistant to the Dean of the College for Latino Affairs, a position that was created that year and that has remained an integral part of Brown University ever since. While in that position, Ricardo became an advocate for Latino students, helping them with cultural, social and academic issues.

However, although he loved his job, Ricardo knew that he hadn't yet found a perfect match for his passion. He thought that becoming involved in another area of academia might offer the answer he was looking for, so he applied to study for a Ph.D. in History at the University of California, in San Diego.

The study of Latin American history gave him great pleasure and the opportunity to explore the reality of a life in academia. "I was very successful writing papers teaching undergrads, and debating other historians but I also discovered that for every one hundred history graduates there were only three positions available in the country and they were often located in places far from my family and cultural roots, such as South Dakota, where I had no desire to live," Ricardo shares.

He also learned that the academic environment was extremely competitive. Professors needed to write grants to get their funding and the competition for even small $5,000 and $10,000 grants was huge.

But an even more crucial fact became evident while exploring the possibility of a life as a History professor: Academia could not provide him with the kind of income he needed in order for him to give his family the opportunities that his classmates at Brown had enjoyed growing up. He wanted to give his children all the opportunities he had never had, and an academic career didn't seem to be the best option for him to accomplish this goal.

At that point, Ricardo seriously wished that he had found somebody along the way who could have helped him understand the job he was preparing himself for. Someone who could have told him that enjoying the educational part of a profession was not enough, that he needed to explore the day-to-day activities involved in the job once he graduated, how much he could expect to be paid, where in the country there was a market for that job and whether that was a place where he'd be comfortable living.

If you look at Ricardo's final choice for a profession, you could say that his detour continued for a few more years, as he became the senior editor of the Center for US/Mexican studies at the University of California, San Diego. But it was while working at this think tank that he met Ralph Reisner, a lawyer who made him think again about studying law. "This man had a very big impact in my life as he described a new area of legal practice: International Law. He talked about lawyers who were helping foreign governments negotiate their external debts with private banks in the U.S. —for example the government of Mexico with Citibank or the government of Brazil with J.P. Morgan. As Mr. Reisner explained the role of the lawyer in these important negotiations, I became increasingly fascinated not just with the issue but also with the fact that there were many jobs available for lawyers. Once I had my degree, I could work in international law or in any other aspect of the law," explains Ricardo.

With this in mind, Ricardo applied and got into Harvard Law School and, upon graduation, he was recruited by Cleary, Gottlieb, Steen and Hamilton, one of the most prestigious law firms in the country. This was one of the firms Reisner had mentioned as being on the forefront of international law. Eight short years later Ricardo Anzaldúa became a partner at the firm, and not long thereafter his annual earnings were in the seven-figure range.

Ricardo was extremely persistent in his search for a good match for his passion and never gave up on the kind of lifestyle he wanted for him and his family. Could he have avoided some delays in his career? Sure! But that's why you are reading this book, so that you can learn from his experience and expand your knowledge to avoid some of the hurdles he had to face.

After seventeen years with Cleary, Gottlieb, Steen and Hamilton, Ricardo left in 2007 to join The Hartford, a large insurance company, to be the Senior VP and Director of Corporate Law.

Ricardo Anzaldúa's Recommendations

✓ Don't ever think you are alone. There is a whole community of professional Latinos who have the same aspirations for you as they had for themselves. There are organizations and advisors who can give you great insight and guidance. Seek them out.

✓ Think carefully about the practical opportunities at the end of your academic career.

✓ In choosing your educational path, make sure you keep in mind not only your intellectual interests, but also the career that will follow. Make sure that you consider whether that degree will allow you to live where you want and enable you to provide for yourself and your family in a way that will be a source of fulfillment and pride *for you,* and certainly not frustration.

Chapter 2

WHEN YOU ARE THE FIRST TO GO TO COLLEGE

Being the first in your family to go to college is a source of great pride but, as Ricardo Anzaldúa's example shows, it can also mean that you will have no role models to follow within your family and that you may have to put up with some conflicting feelings from those around you.

David Peña, Executive Director of the National Hispanic Business Association (www.nhba.org), shares a little bit of that mixed blessing: "Upon my return from college to visit family, there were sudden jokes when I made a mistake. Along the lines of: 'Oh, and that's the college educated one'. I sort of just looked beyond the comments since I knew deep down inside, my family was proud." This is not an unusual experience. Michael G. McKenzie Jr., an Information Technology Analyst at Morgan Stanley who is currently attending Pace University to get his

Masters of Science in Information Systems, says that his relatives in Puerto Rico would always try to downplay his achievements by saying they were not true. "Out of all my cousins that were my age I was the only one that did not have a child at 18 and who was actually graduating from high school and attending college on time but no one would ever really acknowledge me for my accomplishments."

For many people the pressure comes from feeling a big responsibility for being the first to raise the bar to a higher level. The rewards, however, are bigger than anything you can imagine. Jesús José Chávez, Principal, Thomas Jefferson High School at San Antonio Independent School District, in San Antonio, Texas, was the first one in his family to graduate from college. He says: "The emotional feeling of accomplishing a feat never attained by any other family member brought home the reality that upward mobility is possible for anyone."

This is what you have to look forward to when you set your mind to accomplishing a goal that perhaps no one else has ever accomplished in your family. An incredible sense of achievement will accompany you for the rest of your life and that is something nobody can ever take away from you. Those "friends" who tease you about your education will eventually come around to become your biggest supporters or they will soon cease to be your friends. Because, who needs to be around people who don't wish the best for you? As for your family, the most likely outcome is they will feel tremendously proud of you, even if it takes them a little while to come around. It's perfectly normal, and my best advice for you is to be patient. Every parent wishes the best for their children, even if it takes a while for them to understand exactly how it all works.

Advice for Female Students

Sometimes, being a female student presents additional challenges. Lulu Wang, currently a graduate student at Harvard Business School, class of 2010 was born in Venezuela to Chinese parents. Her official name is Ke Yang Wang. She shares her experience: "The pressure that I felt was not from my family but from my circle of friends and their respective families. Most of them thought that it was pointless for me, a woman, to get a higher degree (*machista* culture), when in fact I could contribute to my family's income by finding a job and marrying someone. Thanks to the encouragement from my parents I understood that different people have different perceptions; so I made an extra effort to connect with those who understood my career ambitions and to build my own network of support."

And on this issue, Daisy Auger-Dominguez, Associate Vice President of Diversity at Moody's Corporation and who received her B.A. from Bucknell University and her Master in Public Administration from New York University's Robert F. Wagner Graduate School for Public Policy says: "My biggest challenge was finding my place as a woman of color in a predominantly white institution. As I look back, that experience shaped my cultural identity profoundly and allowed me to be culturally flexible in ways that have certainly helped me personally and professionally."

Being the first to go to college is similar to any situation where you are the first to do something: Whether you create a new club at your high school, or you're the first person in your school to win a national science contest. In a way, if nobody succeeded before you at doing whatever it is you are doing, you will have to create and follow your own path and you will have to contend with people's feelings about it. Sometimes, this responsibility can be a little overwhelming but that doesn't mean you will have to go it alone. You may be the first one in your family to go to college, but you are by no means the first person from a Latino family who does! So, part of what we'll discuss in this book is the importance of finding the people and support systems that Ricardo Anzaldúa failed to come across and who can be your guides and mentors in this exciting journey.

WORDS OF ENCOURAGEMENT

"College is tough for sure. But it's also an amazing journey of self-discovery. The degree will open doors for you but you will have to sell yourself. Make it work for you and be open to the possibilities. Some of the friendships you make in college might be the very ones that open up doors for you in the future. Embrace your new community and build your college family— they will see you through the next four years!"

—Daisy Auger-Dominguez

Let's start from the beginning. What is a mentor?

I often ask this question at workshops and conferences and I'm no longer surprised when just a few people (even amongst mid career employees) can provide an answer. A mentor is someone who guides you in your path whether it's in your educational career or later, in your professional career. It's usually someone who you admire and respect and who is an expert in the area in which you seek guidance.

You may have more than one mentor and they may not stay in your life in the long term, but rather for a specific period in which you need their help. For example, when I was a teenager, I wanted to learn everything I could about being a writer. From the printing of a book to its marketing. So, I looked for mentors in the different areas and I got an internship with a printer, a publisher, a marketing company and so forth. I looked for the best people in the industry and approached them humbly, telling them I wanted to learn their trade. Later, I had several mentors who helped me as I developed my writing career and further honed my skills.

A few years ago, when I began publishing in the U.S., I found a colleague who is now a friend, Marisol González, a producer at HBO sports, who helped me navigate the media circuit so I could be on TV and do segments on the content of my books. She introduced me to several news producers in the Hispanic market who had me as a guest on their shows. That's how I first appeared on Telemundo and Univision. Marisol would go to tapings with me and give me precious feedback once it was over. She would make comments such as: "You should try to keep your head straight when you listen to the interviewer" or "Try not to move your hands so much when you talk", "You need to slow down your speech", etc.

At about the same time, I met another colleague who is also now my friend, Alex Michell, a branding consultant, who helped me in the development of my brand. He and I had long conversations about what I had to offer that was unique about me so that it could become an intrinsic part of my message. It took several meetings to refine my brand so that it would reflect exactly *who* I am and *what* I want to accomplish.

Arturo Poiré, my co-author for *The Latino Advantage in the Workplace*, an expert in Human Resources who at the time we met was a senior executive at Citigroup, has been my career mentor since I interviewed him for my book *How to Get a Job in the U.S.* He has helped me establish short and long term goals as well as understand the best way to work with large corporations. Arturo also spends time with me looking at an idea from different angles so that it has a larger impact when I present it to an audience.

Then I met Julie Stav, a TV and radio personality you may know, who not only invited me as a guest on her radio show but also taught me tons on how to deal with big media corporations and introduced me to her entertainment lawyer so he would help me build my career as a speaker while he protects my legal rights. She also took the time to write a wonderful prologue for the book I co-authored with Arturo Poiré.

As you see, I constantly look for new mentors to guide me along the way, people who are experts in their fields and who can help me in the many different areas I wish to explore. You need to do the same. Look for people who are college graduates, alumni of your college or upper classmen who can reveal the unwritten rules of your particular school, the best way to ace the various courses; the idiosyncrasies of certain professors; the best organizations to join on campus, etc. Throughout this book, you will meet many people whose words can inspire you to find your path. Use them as your virtual mentors until you find your own.

"Don't give up. You will regret it later.
College is tough, however, a successful completion will
overshadow any ill feelings you had along the way.
Once you have completed your studies you will not remember
the sleepless nights, but you will remember your graduation and
what it feels like to make those you love proud."

—Jesús José Chávez, Principal Thomas Jefferson High School,
San Antonio ISD, San Antonio, Texas

You may wish to find successful professionals in your field of interest who may allow you to shadow them at their jobs (or intern in their companies) to get a feel for what it would be like to work in that sector. This will help you avoid a problem Ricardo Anzaldúa often encountered after having invested time and money studying for a particular career: Realizing that the job for which he had studied was not what he had imagined. In the end, the job was only available in a state where he wasn't willing to live, or there were only a few positions available in the country or the job didn't pay enough.

You may also want to find mentors who can help you set up goals and who can introduce you to important contacts. Arturo Poiré, who is now the Senior Vice President/Head of Talent Acquisition at a global financial services company, and as I mentioned before, the co-author of one of my recent books, shares this: "My experience with mentors started during the beginnings of corporate life and I have to admit that it would have made a huge difference to have this type of advice and support before I started."

So, you're probably asking yourself, where do you find mentors? Everywhere around you! Besides the teachers, alumni, and upper classmen, it might be a good idea to join professional associations and attend their conferences and events to meet people in your future profession. Establish relationships with the speakers you will meet at these conferences as well as those who come to your school to teach courses or give presentations. Talk to the many professionals in your life: Your doctor, dentist, banker, lawyer, etc. Remember that you want to choose people who you admire and respect and who are experts in the area in which you seek guidance but it's also important to have some chemistry if you want the relationship to work out. "What is chemistry?" ponders Arturo Poiré. "You have to feel that this person understands what you are going through and can give you unbiased advice (as much as possible); someone who can engage in a dialogue with you. Most people enjoy giving career advice and telling you what they've done and how they've done it. You, however, have to make your own decisions. As a mentor, I don't want to be responsible for the other person's decisions. They have to be accountable for them."

Keep in mind that the mentor/mentee relationship is a two way street. Mentors get a lot of satisfaction from helping people so it's critical that you provide feedback on how their recommendations are helping you and that you express your appreciation for their time and insights. Make sure you keep in touch and you keep them updated on your progress and at the same time, don't hesitate to share your ideas on anything that may help your mentor. You have the great advantage of being young, of knowing your generation and of having a fresh perspective, and these are all things mentors value immensely.

A great place to find mentors are Hispanic-servicing organizations such as the Hispanic Heritage Foundation (www.hispanicheritage.org). They have programs for high school and college students through which they identify emerging young leaders, they provide support, guidance, grants, internships and the opportunity to develop a sustainable relationship with corporations.

There are many other organizations you should look into to find mentors. Hispanic Alliance for Career Enhancement (HACE, www.hace-usa.org) and INROADS (www.inroads.org) are two more examples. You will find them throughout this book and in the resource section of each chapter.

Balancing Family Pressure and
Your Living-Away-From-Home Experience

Because most Latinos have very strong family ties, and because many Latino families are not used to granting their children independence at a young age, moving away from home to go to college may be a struggle for you. If you add to that, the recent violent events at college campuses such as Virginia Tech, your parents have plenty of reasons to fight you on the idea of moving away.

Carla Rivera, a junior at Pace University and a former intern of mine, says that many of the Latino students at her school live on campus from Tuesday to Thursday and they go home Friday through Monday. "They can't socialize and they miss out on one of the most important parts of their college experience. They can't make their presence felt on campus and they miss out on the exposure to different cultures and opportunities, the independence and the growth they could achieve. They stay close to what they know so they don't grow as much as they could. The stereotypes they have about others remain the same."

This is very true and research shows that not living on campus is one of the factors that most affect Latino college graduation rates[2]. If you are living away from home and you are faced with some resistance on behalf of your family, you may need to have a serious conversation with your parents where you express how stressful the situation can become for you, and just how much you will gain from the experience. Below you'll find some suggestions to help you deal with the problem.

Tips On How To Deal With Your Family
When You Are Away In College

Here are some things you can do to get your family onboard:

• Take the time to explain the different aspects of your life in school with as much detail as possible. The less you leave to their imagination, the less they will worry and possibly bother you later. Be specific about the hours you study, the classes you are taking, what a GPA means, the importance of your volunteer work, etc. Also, tell them about your friends and how you spend your free time. This will help them craft a mental image of your new life in college and help appease their concerns.

• Take your parents on a campus visit where they can discuss with the college staff the advantages of moving on campus and where they can be reassured of your well-being. Hearing it from someone other than you will help your parents understand that this decision will be better for you in the long run.

---

[2] "Latino Youth Finishing College: The Role of Selective Pathways," by Richard Fry, Pew Hispanic Center, June 23, 2004.

- Decide early in the school year when you will go back home to visit. This will help reduce their expectations and control their anxiety level. By letting them know ahead of time when you will come back home (and sticking to it) they will feel reassured in that you are not drifting away from your family and your roots.

- Try to figure out what you can do to pay for these return trips yourself. This will take away some of the financial burden, making reunions, all the more joyful.

- Use the information in this book to help them understand what a difference a college degree will make in your future. Explain that people with a college degree earn an average of $1 million more in a lifetime than people without a degree. They also live longer, healthier lives and have much lower unemployment rates than people without a degree. Tell them about success stories you have heard, and share with them your inspiration. The more they understand and are a part of your master plan, the more welcoming they will be of your decisions. While sending you to college might seem daunting right now, it will no doubt be a huge benefit to you and your family in the long run.

- Teach them how to communicate via email and to use Skype and other Voice Over Internet protocols so you can communicate frequently. Send them pictures and share your experience with them as much as you can. There are many ways to remain close despite the distance!

- Clearly tell them that you wish to pursue something that may be outside of what they know, or how things were done up to now in your family. You may want to say something like: "I'm sure that when you came to this country, your parents weren't happy that you were leaving them. But you changed the way in which things were done in your family up to then for a chance of a better future. I'm trying to do the same."

- Openly ask them to support your studies away from home and to avoid telling you repeatedly that you can come back home and study at a local community college if that is not what you chose to do. You can try something like: "Mom, I know you miss me and I miss you too. But I will have so many more opportunities in the future if I stick it out and stay at this college, that I hope you can support my decision. It would really mean a lot to me."

- Find examples of professionals who are well known in your field of interest and talk to your family about them. If you can connect with some of these role models, they can become your inspiration and in some cases, your mentors. This will inevitably contribute to helping your parents see just how serious you are about building your career.

Michael G. McKenzie Jr., the Information Technology Analyst at Morgan Stanley, says: "I went to school at the State University of New York in Potsdam which is six hours away from New York City (where I grew up) by car. I think this was a great experience for me because it got me out of the city environment and exposed me to nature. I also think it helped me get the full college experience of going away and living on campus because it allowed me to open up, meet new people and build relationships, something I think I would not have done if I had gone to school in the city. I feel if I had stayed in the city I would have just gone to class and then got on the train and gone right back home where I would have stayed around my same childhood friends on the corner."

Remember that you create your own path to success one day at a time. By getting your family on your side and by choosing the right people to mentor you and support your growth you are taking very important steps towards your future success. But, as Arturo Poiré reminds you: "You cannot negotiate your future, so, you can show your family statistics about rates of success for college graduates and all that but in the end, you have to realize that it's your future and in this case, as much as your family loves you, if they don't support you, they are not doing you any good."

WORDS OF ENCOURAGEMENT

"As the Executive Director for a national association that represents Hispanic business students across the country I would like to encourage students to go beyond their comfort zone. Attend a university outside of your city and state. Get involved in non-Hispanic traditional activities and/or organizations. Learn and explore what is beyond your family, circle of friends and larger community. What you learn from these experiences will provide you numerous options to seek personally and professionally."

—David Peña

So, if you are the first one in your family to go to college, be proud of being a trailblazer for future generations of people in your family and in the Latino community at large. Realize that even if your family can't guide you through the process, and even if sometimes you have to make decisions despite their lack of support or understanding, you are not alone. On the contrary; there are lots of people out there willing to guide you and help you fulfill your ambitions. You just have to proactively seek their friendship and seek their advice.

One more thing. You can always come back to this book and re-read the Words of Encouragement I peppered throughout these pages. We can all use a little pick me upper once in a while!

Chapter Resources

www.firstinthefamily.org—First in the Family offers a great website where you can find videos and tips for first generation students who are in college.

www.parenthandbook.sa.ucsb.edu—Here you'll find a handbook for parents of first generation students that you can pass on to your family.

www.hispanicfund.org—The Hispanic College Fund is one of the organizations that manages many different scholarships for Hispanics. One of them is The SallieMae Fund's "First in My Family" scholarship for full time undergraduate students enrolled in approved, accredited institutions. More about scholarships in Chapter 5.

www.100hispanicwomen.org—This organization helps young Latinas become leaders by providing them mentorship, networking and internship opportunities.

www.imno.org—A virtual mentoring organization that invites college students to interview people they admire and then post the audio file on the website.

www.nextgeneratinpress.org—A website where you can download the complete PDF of the book *First In the Family* by Kathleen Cushman.

www.gotocollege.wikispaces.com/advice+for+1st+generation+college+students—Offers a list of websites with articles for first generation college students.

www.hace-usa.org—Hispanic Alliance for Career Enhancement offers a mentoring program for high school and college students. In addition they have a high school internship program that identifies top performers for exposure to the corporate world.

www.hispanicheritage.org—Hispanic Heritage Foundation identifies, supports and develops high school students and recent college graduates by offering opportunities to connect with corporations and to get involved with the community.

Books

First In the Family: Your High School Years: Advice About College From First Generation Students, by Kathleen Cushman (Paperback, 2006).

I Am Somebody: College Knowledge For the First Generation Campus Bound, by Anna J. Leider (Octameron, 1998).

I Am Somebody: College Knowledge For at Risk Students, 16th edition, by Anna J. Leider (Octameron, 2000).

Foundations: A Reader For New College Students by Virginia Gordon and Thomas L. Minnick (Paperback, 2007).

For more information and a constantly updated list of resources log on to **www.latinosincollege.com**.

Chapter 3

PREPARE FOR THE CAREERS OF THE FUTURE

Choosing the right college for you has a lot to do with what your interests are. Some people know early on that they want to be lawyers, doctors or scientists, while others take longer to recognize their passion and talent. If you are still in high school you have a big advantage: You get to explore the careers that offer the best opportunities in the future. Finding out early that you'd like to work in technology, for instance, will enable you to take the right courses now, while you still have time. Let's look at how that works.

Here are a few questions for you: Do you know what you'd like to study? Do you even know what intrigues you? Have you taken any of the interest inventory tests that are available in most high schools, such as Coin, Choices or Discover? If you haven't, ask your guidance counselor for a password to access the website and take the test. It will give you a variety of careers that might pique your interest.

There is no question about the fact that you need to take a long look at yourself to try to figure out what you would like to do. And a good place to start is with what you are good at, what activities you enjoy. There are books that can guide you in this soul-searching process and I'll give you some of them in the Resources at the end of the chapter.

Another good idea is to take a look at the Occupational Outlook Handbook (OOH) at www.bls.gov/oco. This wonderful directory published by the Federal Government offers a list of every single imaginable occupation in the United States along with a description of what the job entails, what kind of education you need, what the average salary is and the projected growth of that job in the future. You will discover careers you didn't even imagined that existed! In addition you will find a link on the OOH's website called "Jobs of the Future" where you can search by looking at the fastest growing industries.

Unfortunately, in the past several years, not enough students are choosing to get on the pathway to an engineering, technological or science career, perhaps because they don't see the kinds of careers they could have if they follow the so called STEM field, Science, Technology, Engineering and Math.

Yine de la Cruz, Project Engineer at ExxonMobil Fuels Marketing, who recently graduated with a Bachelor of Science in Civil Engineering from Manhattan College, decided to take the road less traveled: At the advice of her guidance counselor in school, she took every available course in the math and science departments in her high school. "The truth is, that by choosing a heavy work load in high school I was more than prepared for anything that I faced in college. My first Calculus class was a review of all the material I had learned in high school.

Thus, I had a head start and felt confident in my abilities to succeed in the engineering program." she says.

Not having the right preparation by the time you get to college might close important doors for you as some interesting options may be out of reach. In addition, not being able to choose a promising career path will not only impact your future; it will also impact the future of our country. Why? Because the fact that we have entered the era of globalization and are rapidly advancing through the information age, has increased the demand for employees with higher technological skills. For instance, it is estimated that in the next ten years, half a million engineers will retire and we will need an additional half a million to fulfill market demand. Yet, the U.S. is only graduating around 70,000 engineers a year. Do you see now that there is great need for more students to take advantage of this opportunity?

Yine's determination and a clear understanding of her goals early on, allowed her to tap into key resources which she leveraged once she graduated.

As her family had limited financial means and couldn't afford to pay for college, Yine applied to several scholarships and received the Exxon-Mobil Math and Engineering Award through the Hispanic Heritage Foundation, an organization that identifies, supports and develops emerging Latino leaders. (This award totaled $22,000 for four years plus a laptop.)

While in school, Yine interned at STV, Inc., a company that offered engineering, architectural, planning and construction management services, and she received a job offer from them upon graduation. A few months later, however, Yine was invited to talk to young students at the Hispanic Heritage Foundation gala. There, she reconnected with Nicolás Medina, one of ExxonMobil's representatives who recognized her from the ceremony at which she had received her award a few years earlier. He asked her to interview with his company. "I didn't know much about the corporate world and he took the time to talk to me about career development and job opportunities and many other things I had quite honestly never learned in college or at home."

After a series of interviews with ExxonMobil, Yine de la Cruz was offered a project manager position.

As Yine's example shows, if you wish to stay ahead of the game, you need to seriously explore where the greatest employment growth will be in the next few years and try to match that information with your interests and talents. Then, you need to look for the best schools to prepare you for the challenge and you need to find available resources for your area of interest.

Here are some insights on future career trends as described on the Occupational Outlook Handbook, 2008-09 Edition:

- Healthcare and social assistance—This sector is expected to grow by 25.4 percent and add nearly 4 million jobs due to an aging population and longer life expectancy. Seven of the 20 fastest growing occupations are expected to be in healthcare. There will be a great need for medical assistants, registered nurses, substance abuse and behavioral disorder counselors, health care aids, mental health and substance abuse social workers, etc.

- Professional and business services—This super sector, which includes some of the fastest growing industries in the country, is expected to grow by 23.3 percent and add 4.1 million new jobs. Jobs with high levels of growth will be computer and mathematical occupations, healthcare practitioners, technical occupations, education and training.

- Professional, scientific and technical services—This sector will grow by 28.8 percent adding an estimated 2.1 million new jobs by 2016.

Employment in computer systems, design and related services will grow by 38.3 percent and add nearly one-fourth of all new jobs in this sector. Management, scientific and technical consulting services will grow at a 78 percent. Demand for these services will be spurred by the increased use of new technology and computer software and the growing complexity of business. There will be a need for: systems analyst, designers and developers, computer programmers, web developers, information managers, software and hardware engineers.

• Public and private educational services—This sector will grow by 10.7 percent and add around 1.4 million new jobs by 2016. This is due to the rising student enrollment at all levels of education. Teachers will be needed in all areas, particularly in math, science and technology.

Percent Change in Employment in Occupations Projected to Grow Fastest, 2006-2016

✓ Network systems and data communications analysts

✓ Personal and home care aides

✓ Home health aides

✓ Computer software engineers, applications

✓ Veterinary technologists and technicians

✓ Personal financial advisors

✓ Makeup artists, theatrical performance

✓ Medical assistants

✓ Veterinarians

✓ Substance abuse and behavioral disorder counselors

✓ Skin care specialists

✓ Financial analysts

✓ Social and human service assistants

✓ Gaming surveillance officers and gaming investigators

✓ Physical therapist assistants

✓ Pharmacy technicians

✓ Forensic science technicians

✓ Dental hygienists

✓ Mental health counselors

✓ Mental health and substance abuse social workers

Source: U.S. Bureau of Labor Statistics, Occupational Outlook Handbook, 2008-09 Edition.

Another industry where Latinos need to continue to gain ground is the financial markets. It's a field you may not know much about and something that your parents may not have encouraged you to do, not because they are against you working at a Wall Street firm, but because they many not be aware of how Wall Street can influence the well being of millions of people. Yes, I know that the recent Wall Street collapse has probably made a strong impact on the way you see the industry. But the truth is that you could bring a different perspective and help shape the way in which this sector conducts its business.

Mina Pacheco Nazemi is the Vice President of the private equity division of alternative investments at Credit Suisse, and one of the highest-ranking Latinas in her company. She graduated from Stanford University with honors with a degree in Economics and Political Science and has an MBA from Harvard Business School. She shares how her work makes a big impact in the community: "Wall Street is about supporting and financing companies to help them expand, grow or meet their ongoing capital needs. Wall Street firms have not traditionally invested in minority businesses. Among the challenges in investing behind minority firms has been a 'people issue.' Wall Street firms and asset managers work with people they know. They finance deals that are brought to their attention. It is much more difficult for a minority company to get the attention of a financier if they do not have the relationship or connections. The research shows that management teams with women and minorities tend to hire more women and minorities and manage companies that operate in these communities. These businesses provide economic development in their communities. With billions of dollars available for investment but few Latinos in Wall Street managing those funds, this capital will have a harder time being funneled down to Latino businesses and hence Latino communities. So, getting into finance is a great way to contribute to the development of your community."

Mina's work has a strong multiplying effect. She just raised $300 million from one of the largest institutional investors in the country to be invested behind women and minority-owned businesses. By choosing every investment carefully, she can ensure that the capital is being designated to businesses (and managers) that are women or minority-owned.

The best way to get your foot in the door at a Wall Street firm is through an internship. Mina was initially exposed to Wall Street through an organization called Sponsors for Educational Opportunity (SEO) **www.seo-usa.org**. They recruit the best minority students from all over the country and place them in internships at leading Wall Street firms. This program does more than just place you in an internship, it also exposes you to high-ranking executives at receptions and it prepares you to interact with them. It actually provides you a network, a "family" of other minorities on Wall Street. If you look at the minorities in Wall Street, about 80 percent of them are graduates of the SEO program.

Mina, a board member of this organization, shares: "The SEO program is your training ground to learn what Wall Street is; it teaches you accounting, financial analysis, and gives you the skill sets needed to become a good investor. Before the start of your internship you go through a rigorous training process to make sure each intern is well equipped to succeed. And more importantly it provides you with an invaluable network that will aid your success on the Street."

Occupations with the Largest Numerical Growth, by Level of Postsecondary Education

Bachelor's degree

- ✓ Elementary school teachers
- ✓ Accountants and auditors
- ✓ System engineers, applications
- ✓ System analysts
- ✓ Secondary school teachers
- ✓ System engineers, software
- ✓ System administrators
- ✓ Intermediate school teachers
- ✓ Human resources specialists

Bachelor's or higher degree plus work experience

- ✓ Management analysts
- ✓ Financial managers
- ✓ Computer and information systems managers
- ✓ Medical and health service managers
- ✓ Training and development specialists

Master's degree

- ✓ Clergy
- ✓ Physical therapists
- ✓ Mental health and substance abuse social workers
- ✓ Educational, vocational and school counselors
- ✓ Rehabilitation counselors

Doctoral degree

- ✓ Postsecondary teachers
- ✓ Clinical, counseling and school psychologists
- ✓ Medical scientists
- ✓ Computer and information scientists
- ✓ Biochemists and biophysicists

Source: U.S. Bureau of Labor Statistics, Occupational Outlook Handbook, 2008-09 Edition.

Some students think that math, science and technology are boring subjects, yet they couldn't fathom their lives without products and services created and developed by people who dedicate their careers to these areas.

Think about it for a minute: TIVO, all MP3 players, the Wii and XBOX 360 consoles, as well as your favorite social networks such as Facebook and My Space; You Tube, iTunes, Google and all the other search engines were all invented by scientists and engineers. The fact that you can download your favorite ringtone to your cell phone and that you can use your cell phone to navigate the Internet, text your friends and purchase jeans off a billboard (soon to be available in the U.S.!) is all thanks to people who took advanced high school math classes (such as trigonometry and calculus) that are prerequisites for admission to competitive colleges and for career success. Interesting, isn't it? That your choice of courses in high school can make such a difference in your career path, in your future and in the level of success you achieve. Remember, no matter where you are in your studies, it's never too late to start thinking about the possible career choices available to you.

WORDS OF ENCOURAGEMENT

Yine de la Cruz, engineer at ExxonMobil says:

"The world of engineering is filled with opportunities and there is nothing but room to grow for any Latinos entering the field. The fact is that the country needs a more diverse group of engineers with ideas that could revolutionize science and the practical world of today. My favorite quote of all time is: 'Knowledge is power'. That's how I feel about an engineering background: it's a problem solving skill not just merely a profession. Thus, having the skill to approach problems in an organized way, following processes and arriving at productive conclusions could get you any job. Engineers could be bankers, financial analysts, scientists, teachers and any other profession that requires the skill to learn and to solve problems. At this point in my life I am positive that the best way to solve problems on the spot and to think critically is by expanding your mind. Treat your mind as you would any muscle. If you want tighter abs, do sit-ups. If you want to become a better intellectual, push yourself to think outside the box. Begin thinking on your own.

Don't stop at completing your homework tasks. Go above and beyond. I truly think that pursuing a degree in an engineering field is the best way to helping you achieve this goal."

CHAPTER RESOURCES

www.seo-usa.org—Sponsors of Educational Opportunity—An organization that provides support in grades 9-16 by preparing students of color for competitive college admissions and graduation. Their SEO Career Program recruits, selects and trains college students of color for summer internships that lead to full time jobs with investment banks, corporate law firms and other leading global companies. They have several other programs you should look into.

www.nationalmathandscience.org—National Math and Science Initiative—This organization was formed to address one of America's greatest economic and intellectual problems: The declining number of student who are prepared to take rigorous college courses in math and science and equipped for careers in those fields. It's a public-private partnership led by private donors such as ExxonMobil Corporation, the Bill and Melinda Gates Foundation and the Michael and Susan Dell Foundation. Visit the site to find out how you can benefit from their programs.

www.hispanicheritage.org—Hispanic Heritage Foundation—This organization identifies, promotes and prepares Latino role models through national leadership, cultural, educational and workforce programs. They offer programs such as: the Hispanic Heritage Youth Awards which annually identifies and honors youth role models in various categories from 12 regions in the country; LOFT (Latinos on Fast Track) Workforce Program, which was created in partnership with Hispanic College Fund to identify and prepare emerging Latino professionals in specific industries or jobs; and the Hispanic Heritage Awards, which is one of the most prestigious Hispanic awards events recognizing successful Latinos in various categories.

Books

What Color Is Your Parachute for Teens: Discovering Yourself, Defining Your Future by Richard Nelson Bolles, Carol Christen, and Jean M. Blomquist. (Ten Speed Press, 2006).

If You Could Be Anything, What Would You Be? A Teen Guide to Mapping Out the Future by Jeanne Webster (Paperback, 2004).

For more information and a constantly updated list of resources log on to **www.latinosincollege.com**.

Chapter 4

CHOOSING THE RIGHT SCHOOL FOR YOU

One of the key decisions you have to make in your life is where to go to college. It has so many implications for your future that taking the time to research your options is crucial. Granted, you can do all the research in the world and still find out that you picked the wrong school regardless of how great it looked on paper. But the chances of this happening will be greatly reduced

When looking at college, you have to take into account a number of things, from attending a community college, a trade school or a four-year college or university, to applying for a highly selective or an open doors policy institution, to going away to school or staying close to home, to trying for a private college or a public school. And there are also statistics that you may want to look at. Dr. Antonio R. Flores, President and CEO of the Hispanic Association of Colleges and Universities

(HACU) says that the main factors a Latino student should evaluate before choosing a college are social and cultural fit, field of study chosen, and the graduation rates, especially those of Hispanic students.

There is one other aspect that I know you and your family will consider very seriously: What you can afford. And an important aspect it is. So before we go any further, let's take a moment to look into the financial aspects of going to college.

Can You Afford College?

The question should not be whether you can afford college or not, but rather what would the cost be of not going to the best college you are able to qualify for. Because you see, there are all different kinds of schools and we will look at them in a minute, but the truth is that many Latino families only look at a limited number of them based on how much they cost or which ones are close to home. You should be looking at colleges because they are excellent for your field of study, because they have a fantastic reputation and they are a good match for you, not because they are cheap or nearby.

Now you are probably asking yourself: "How can I not take into consideration the cost of a college?" So let me tell you. Most Latinos grow up thinking it's bad to borrow money. They believe that you should pay cash for what you want and avoid debt at all costs. And don't get me wrong: As a Latina I agree with the underlying philosophy that one should never spend beyond one's means and in fact, this country would be in much better shape if more people lived by such rules, as it has recently been proven with the market meltdown of 2008. But, forgoing a great college education because you don't want to borrow money, is not only silly: It will seriously limit your future opportunities.

See, although having a college degree is much better than not having a degree at all, all college degrees are not made equal. Depending on your career, employers tend to hire students from certain universities and having a degree from particular schools will open a lot more doors than having a degree from less reputable colleges. In addition, the opportunities that top colleges afford you have a lot to do not just with the level of education they provide but also the caliber of contacts you can develop there.

More importantly: The level of selectivity of the institution is tightly correlated to the college graduation rate. This means that attending a highly selective college will offer you a better chance at graduating with a Bachelor's degree than attending open enrollment institutions.[3] And contrary to popular belief, it doesn't necessarily cost more to study at highly selective colleges because they are usually better endowed than less selective institutions and they have the ability to subsidize low-income students. So read on!

My suggestion then, is that you look at all the best schools that match your interests and personality. Next look at what they offer you in terms of financial aid. Try to get as much scholarship money as you can and then get a government-subsidized loan to pay for the difference. We will look at this issue in detail later in the book.

---

[3] "Latino Youth Finishing College: The Role of Selective Pathways," by Richard Fry, Pew Hispanic Center, June 23, 2004.

*"Education is an investment you will never regret.
You can make money, have a nice car, or a nice house and it
can all be taken away. Even your freedom can be taken away,
but nobody can take away your education."*

—Gregorio Hallman Jr., a doctoral student at Teacher's College,
Columbia University, New York City

College Night or College Fair

One of the great ways to find out about colleges is to attend the College Night or College Fair organized by your high school during your junior and your senior years. There you will have a chance to meet with admissions counselors who are experts in their college and ask them all sorts of questions. It's important to take your parents with you so they share on the experience and get even more excited about you going to college.

Visiting Colleges

If you are in high school you are probably getting tons of colorful brochures from colleges all over the country. Look carefully through each one to familiarize yourself with the different schools and then try to arrange visits to the ones that look interesting. If there's a budget issue in terms of travel cost, keep in mind that nowadays, most colleges offer virtual tours on their websites. And although nothing can substitute for the feeling you can get at the actual campus (where you get to also meet students and faculty), taking the virtual tour will give you a very good idea of what to expect.

Types of Post Secondary Education

I'm sure that if you're reading this book you already know how crucial it is to get an education beyond high school, or what we call post-secondary education. In the next few years most of the jobs will require it as a minimum education standard. Let's look at the different options available to you.

A. Vocational Training School

This type of school offers practical training focused on a specific area. For instance: paralegal training, cosmetology programs, automotive training, medical billing, etc. They are usually privately owned institutions, although some states offer programs as well. Vocational schools offer shorter programs (starting with programs that last a few months) that prepare you to work in a specific field but they provide limited academic education. They offer a quick solution to finding a job by preparing you to work at positions that are in high demand.

Although this may look like a great way to get a job sooner, be aware that you will be limiting your career choices. If your current life situation doesn't allow you to attend a four-year college, you may want to look into this option. Keep in mind that there is no reason for this to be the end of the educational road for you. With a strong determination, you can always make your way back to school.

Before you select a vocational school, make sure that it's accredited (check its accrediting institutions on the U.S. Education Department's website: www.us.edu and on the Council for Higher Education Accreditation's website: www.chea.org.) Also, make sure it's a reputable school.

If your goal is to get a job as soon as possible, you may be able to take trade-related courses and complete fully degreed careers online. Check the Chapter Resources section for some well-known online universities.

WORDS OF ENCOURAGEMENT

Louis Maldonado, account executive at
D'Exposito and Partners, a public relations agency, shares:
*"I would obviously stay true to your desires and dreams
but listen to your parents and mentors because they have lived
and experienced and have learned much along the way.
They may not have the same type of experiences but they have
acquired transferable knowledge and wisdom. Know that
more likely than not they have your best interests at heart.
Try to understand where they are coming from and keep an
open stream of conversation so that they can better understand
your ideas and position and how to best guide you. Finally,
embrace any opportunity to learn or experience something new,
and pursue these opportunities con gusto! You'll get much more
out of it in the end and you will impact and/or influence
others in ways you've never imagined possible."*

B. Community College

A community or junior college (also called county colleges in some states) offers a two-year Associate's degree (60 general education credits) and it may be a great way to transition from high school to a four-year college. They are much cheaper than four-year institutions, so many people choose to fulfill their general education credits at a community college and then transfer to a four-year school. If you decide to go this route, make sure that the credits you take are transferable to the four-year college you plan to attend.

Attending a community college may be a good idea if you're unsure of what you'd like to study, if you have to live at home for a couple of years or if you just want to save money. Because they have an open enrollment policy, community colleges are also a good option if you didn't do that well in high school or if you dropped out and then obtained your GED. Without a doubt, this is one of the biggest advantages of enrolling in a community college so remember, no matter how you have done in your studies up until now, you can always go back to school and get a degree. The right level of discipline and hard work will get you right back on track to achieve your educational and professional goals.

Other things to keep in mind when attending a community college are:

• Most students in a community college commute to school therefore making it difficult to coordinate study groups or participate in extracurricular activities.

• As a consequence of most students not living on campus, the social aspect of college is basically lost, something that may affect your ability to build a strong network for the future.

For more information on community colleges i be sure to check out the next chapter.

C. Four-Year Colleges

The bulk of this chapter is dedicated to four-year colleges because I believe this is the option that you need to think about the most in order to make the right decision. It might seem like the most difficult option, but as you will see, it is definitely worth the effort. The benefits you will reap are innumerable.

While you read this material, remember that choosing the right college is ultimately a balancing act. You will have to factor in several elements such as the level of diversity on campus, the fact that the school is strong in your area of interest, that it has a good reputation, that is a good fit for you and that you feel you can afford it. And let's not forget the decision of staying close to home or moving away. So let's dive in.

1. Public or Private

Public colleges are supported and operated by the individual states and because they are funded by state tax dollars they are generally less expensive than private colleges. They also have special rates for students who are residents of the state.

Undocumented Students—Check This Out!

If you happen to be an undocumented student, there are several states that charge in-state tuition to undocumented students who live in the state. These states are: California, Illinois, Kansas, New Mexico, New York, Oklahoma, Texas, Utah and Washington. Unfortunately, the remaining states charge undocumented students out-of-state tuition even if they live in the state.

In general, being undocumented is not an impediment to enroll in college. It only becomes an issue when you need financial aid. As students who are undocumented don't qualify for federal financial aid, you shouldn't be filling out FAFSA applications or other forms to request this type of aid. If this is your case and you are a very good student, consider applying to a private university. Given that they have private endowments, they may choose to provide financial aid to you regardless of your immigration status. Don't give up! There is *always* an option. You might just have to work a little harder at finding it.

You may choose to go to a public university in your state or outside of your state (which will cost you, according to a 2002 study by the College Board, an average of $6,347 more).

Residency requirements vary from state to state but some of the most typical ones include:

- A durational residency requirement, which tends to be around 12 months.

- The intent to be a permanent resident for the foreseeable future.

The college, however, has the right to determine if you qualify or not as a state resident so you should be prepared to provide proof of residency. Proof usually include:

- Local bank account

- A driver's license issued by the state

- Records of attending high school in the state

- Car or voter registration

To find out the residency requirements of the state where you are interested in applying visit the College Board's website (www.college-board.com) to read their Guide to State Residency Requirements.

There is something else you should know. If you are in a certain geographic area and are interested in programs not available at the state universities in your home state, you may be eligible for one of the tuition-exchange programs through which you'd be charged in-state tuition (even if you're not a resident of the state) or a reduced tuition. To find out the special restrictions on reenrollment that apply, you need to check with the individual schools. See the Chapter Resources section for the websites of the different exchange programs and the participating states.

One last thing to keep in mind when thinking of state universities is that they tend to have large enrollments, large classes and less personal attention. Read below to see the advantages and disadvantages of big schools.

Student to Student

Paloma I. Veloz, a senior student at Syracuse University, Syracuse, New York, shares her experience of being Latina in college: "Going away to school was a big cultural shock for me. I sometimes let the ignorance of some people bring me down. With time, though, I learned that a lot of people don't necessarily come from a diverse community and their comments and actions are just a reflection of that. Many classmates wouldn't think twice to ask me where I was from, because of my accent. I used to take this as an offense because I felt some people were more interested in figuring out my background than getting to know me as a person. I became a little self conscious of my accent and started to think of it as a flaw. Nonetheless, I realized that the only one bringing me down was myself, because I was letting people's comments get to me. I came to embrace my accent as something that makes me different than most people. It's a part of who I am and how far I've come to reach my dreams!"

2. Private Universities

Private universities are not funded by the state government, so they are usually more expensive. But don't think that just because they are more expensive they are off-limits to you. In fact, private institutions tend to offer more scholarships and grants. As a matter of fact, there is a movement started by the Ivy League schools to pay 100 percent of the tuition and expenses for students whose parents have an income that falls below certain level. For example, at Harvard University, the expected contribution of a family making less than $60,000 is **zero**! This university is replacing student loans by grants and is inspiring many other universities both large and small to increase the financial aid they offer to their students. So, don't count the top schools out just because you think they are very expensive and your family can't afford them. If you have a great academic record, you should consider applying to the best schools in the country. There is a strong chance that you will be accepted.

Ivy League Schools

This is the list of the eight U.S. universities (and their acceptance rate) that comprise what it's known as the Ivy League, a small group of private universities that have a reputation for providing excellent education and for attracting the best students.

Brown ....13.5 percent
Columbia ....10.4 percent
Cornell ....20.5 percent
Dartmouth ....14 percent
Harvard ....9 percent
Penn..15.9 percent
Princeton ....9.5 percent
Yale ....9.6 percent

Figures are for the Fall 2007 entering class.

Keep in mind what I said earlier: The highly selective schools have a higher graduation rate than less selective schools.

3. The Level of Diversity of The Institution

If being within a multicultural group feels more comfortable to you, you should look at the diversity of the student population, the faculty and of course the curriculum. Are there enough activities to interest a wide variety of students? Are there enough clubs and courses that reflect different points of view? Remember, attending a school where you are one of only a handful of Latinos may be difficult, but it doesn't have to be impossible. So, when checking out a campus, pay special attention to how you feel amongst its students. Do you get a sense that your cultural background and viewpoint will be reflected in the curriculum? Do you feel the atmosphere is inclusive enough of your differences? Make sure to talk to students and faculty and feel free to ask questions about their experience in campus.

Dr. Antonio R. Flores, President and CEO of the Hispanic Association of Colleges and Universities (HACU), says: "There tends to be two very different types of institutions. Those with large Latino enrollment—generally identified as Hispanic Serving Institutions or HSIs—and those with low Latino enrollment, which are usually more selective (Ivy League type schools, for example). HSIs have fewer resources to serve students with greater needs than those at selective institutions and thus have lower graduation rates. HSIs with 25 percent or greater Hispanic enrollment, enroll and graduate the majority of all Hispanics in college." Dr. Flores explains that more selective institutions enroll and graduate fewer Hispanics but percentage-wise, their graduation rates are slightly higher because of the better academic preparation and socioeconomic status of their Latino students along with the greater resources they have.

If there is a good number of Latinos on campus, make sure you explore what the community is like. At times, Latinos can discriminate amongst each other making it as hard to fit in (if you are from the underrepresented group), as it is in a school with few Latinos around. So make sure you take the time to meet other Latino students and get a feel for what the atmosphere is like.

As only one of the very few Mexican-Americans on campus, Carla Rivera, a California-born junior at Pace University in New York, has felt looked down upon by the Dominican majority from the first day of school. "It was very surprising and hurtful to me. Because on this side

of the country Latinos think that Mexicans are the lowest of the low."
She hasn't let that deter her, however, from her involvement with the
Latino community and with her goal of bringing more Latinos to campus so they can all feel more support. "When I was applying to college,
I looked at [different colleges'] websites to find out what their student
body looked like: How many students where local, how many from out
of state, how many lived on campus... I wanted a school that had a fair
amount of Latinos, African Americans and Asians," says Carla. For her,
that which was a priority in the beginning, took a back seat to the fact
that she found a college near New York City (another one of her priorities) and it had the kind of campus-feel she wanted. She wanted to
experience the school spirit at sports events and the like. Pace was small
and it had a big football field, "something you can only find in a university like Columbia in New York," Carla explains.

WORDS OF ENCOURAGEMENT

"Never doubt how good you are.
Give the best of you, be the best you can be and
you'll be fine. Have passion and love for what you do.
Always behave in a professional manner.
Never give up no matter how tough the road gets.
Hang in there. Once you get to the top
you will enjoy the view!"

—Marisela Riveros, senior TV producer

4. The Size and Location of the School

Some people prefer things small while others go for big. When you consider the right fit for you, you have to look at the size of the school as one of the determining factors. Both big and small schools have advantages and disadvantages and only by being aware of them will you be able to decide which would make more sense for you.

Let's look at some of the pros and cons of big colleges and universities . . .

Pros

- Wide range of majors and courses to choose from
- Large diversity of students
- Wide range of activities both social and academic (many clubs, organizations on campus, cultural activities, events, parties, lectures)
- Well-funded libraries and research facilities
- Well-funded sports programs (also, school spirit)
- Distinguished faculty (large lecture halls where you can meet lots of people)
- A variety of housing options
- Important guest speakers
- Many people in town are affiliated with the university
- Good transportation system catered to students

Cons

- Anonymity: You can get lost in the crowd
- Large class size
- Little interaction with students

- Little connection with professors
- Many courses are taught by teaching assistants
- Long lines everywhere (from cars at the gate on move-in day to people lining up to pay at the bookstore)
- Long distances between campus buildings
- More red tape associated with choosing courses

A big school can be very exciting if you are an outgoing, go-getter type of person and you know what you want to study. It's an environment where you will succeed if you speak up and participate and if you don't feel intimidated by crowds. It is also a wonderful place to meet people from all different backgrounds and it's more likely to have a larger number of Latinos on campus. If you grew up in a large city and you went to a large high school and you enjoyed the experience, this may be a good fit for you. If you come from a small community and went to a small high school and you feel you'd like to open up your choices, then a big school may also be good for you. Be aware, however, that if this is your background, a big school may feel intimidating and you may feel lost. Let's hear Carla Rivera's point of view on this: "I had heard from friends of mine who were attending big state schools that they felt like a number. They felt their professors didn't even know they were sitting in class. I didn't want that. I wanted a college where I could establish a relationship with my professors and with other students so I didn't apply to any school with more than 10,000 students."

Here are some pros and cons of small colleges . . .

Pros

- Small classes

- Strong personal relationships with advisors, teachers and students
- Most courses are taught by professors
- Opportunity to design your own major
- Hands-on learning opportunities
- Strong sense of community

Cons

- Less variety of majors to choose from
- Fewer resources and opportunities (less library and research resources, fewer physical resources, fewer social opportunities, etc.)
- Less focus on sports
- Limited housing options

A small school will work for you if you feel better in small groups (if you are shy or more introspected) and if you enjoy a high level of interaction with your professors. It is also an ideal place if you wish to pursue an individual major focused on a specific area of interest.

If you grew up in a small community where you knew all your neighbors by name and you went to a small high school, attending a small college may feel more familiar to you, even though it won't offer you a new experience, the way a big school would. If you are more of an introvert and feel safer in a more intimate environment, this kind of school may work well for you.

When you look at the size of the school, you should also look at the location. Is it set in a big city where there are lots of things to do? Or is it in a remote location where you have to drive an hour to get to the closest town? Here are some pros and cons of the location of a school that you should consider:

Urban Schools

Pros

- Greater diversity of people and culture
- Wide range of activities (entertainment, cultural, social)
- Wide range of internship opportunities
- Generally, good public transportation (saves you from needing a car)
- Usually, near airports

Cons

- Increased number of distractions
- Generally, less safe
- Generally, more expensive
- Less access to outdoor activities
- Less sense of a community as many students are commuters
- Less opportunity to find study groups as many students work and have a tough schedule outside of school

Jennifer L. Quijano, a student at Brooklyn College, a large urban school says: "I have found that attending a large urban school has really increased my ability to act as an individual. It's a commuter school so everyone usually attends class and then goes home. It seems very few are involved in student life, and the school itself doesn't promote many group activities. This has been a good thing and a bad thing. It's beneficial because I've learned a great deal about myself. I have grown and learned to fend for myself. On the other hand, I feel a sense of community is important and I have not found that in my school experience."

So, as I said before, it's always about balancing your goals and needs with what a school offers. An urban school will give you the city experience but it will limit your involvement with other students and the benefits you can derive from that.

Rural Schools

Pros

- A strong sense of community
- Easier access to outdoor activities
- Less distractions
- High interaction with professors
- Safe environment

Cons

- Less diversity in the community
- Fewer options for internships
- Small range of activities available (social, cultural, etc.)
- Usually not near airports

A rural campus offers a secluded life, far from the noise, the traffic and other distractions of a city. If you like the outdoors, this may be a great option for you. Because the school is the center of academic and social life, they tend to offer a tight sense of community and a high level of interaction with the professors. They also tend to be a safe environment, something that will put your parents at ease.

Keep in mind that not all urban campuses are the same. Some are large and expand over several blocks while others are small. Some are set in the middle of the city while others are set in a separate area. These differences will impact your college experience so make sure that you take them into consideration when you are looking at which schools you might like to attend.

WORDS OF ENCOURAGEMENT

*"In your life you might find a few people that are
very successful without having a college education; they may
be friends, family members, neighbors, even in the press you
might read about college dropouts who became billionaires like
Michael Dell, Bill Gates, or Mark Zuckerberg (they founded
Dell computers, Microsoft and Facebook). Don't let those
few examples lure you away from the best way to increase your
possibilities to achieve middle-class and beyond!!!!
Even if a college education is not a guarantee of success,
the number of successful people in our world who don't have
higher education is VERY small. Look at the statistics,
not individual cases. By getting a college degree, you will do
yourself the greatest favor that you can, as well as doing
it for your current and your future family!"*

—Miguel R. Olivas-Luján, Ph.D., Professor of
Management at Clarion University of Pennsylvania

5. Academic Offering

A great way to evaluate the academic focus of different colleges is by considering the percentage of students by major. Some colleges have just one particular focus. For example the Massachusetts Institute of Technology (MIT) specializes in science and technology so they offer a smaller number of liberal arts courses than other universities.

A specialized college offers a large selection of courses related to your field and more research opportunities than colleges that don't have an area of specialization. Most students have the same kind of time-consuming schedule, whereas in a non-specialized college your curriculum may be more demanding than that of a student with a different major. This difference may prove distracting to those with a more demanding course load but at the same time, sharing a campus with students who are studying all sorts of things will likely make your experience more interesting and diverse.

As with the other aspects that you should look into when considering what the best college is for you, choosing a specialized college or a non-specialized one depends on your goals. If you already have a clear idea of what you want to study and the area you'd like to focus on, then perhaps a specialized college is best for you. But if you are still unsure of what you think you want your major to be, or if you are interested in several different disciplines that are very different from each other (say, biology, literature and history, for example) then a non-specialized school is probably your best bet.

6. Staying Close to Home or Moving Away for College

Above and beyond the size of the school, the location, level of diversity and academic offering, you need to think about whether you want to experience living away from home during your college years or if you wish to live at home and attend a college nearby.

For the past couple of years, I've been conducting parent to teach parents what they can do while their children are in high school in order to help them go to college. Every time I ask participants to raise their hand if they wish for their kids to go to college near home almost 100 percent of the attendees raise their hands. What does this tell you? That it's very likely that your parents will also feel this way.

Families that come from Latin America are not used to giving their children the level of independence that American kids get so early on. They tend to be more protective and controlling, making it hard for them to think about letting you go away for school. But the truth is that your best opportunity may not be near your home.

When you consider all the options available to you, think about how living on campus makes it easier for you to study and concentrate, because the fact is, it tends to be everyone else's priority. It's easier to find people who can help you with things you don't understand, and it's also easier to arrange to study in groups because everyone lives close to each other. You'll probably feel a stronger sense of community and belonging as it's all about school, team spirit, etc. When you live either in an apartment off campus or at home, you feel less of a sense of community and it becomes harder to hook up with other students to study because every one has different priorities and schedules.

Finally, if you decide to go away to college and you are getting some family opposition, please review the ideas I offered in Chapter 1.

CHAPTER RESOURCES

www.collegenight.com—A monthly newsletter guide to your college selection plus a lot of wonderful resources.

www.collegeboard.com—You will find here articles about pros and cons of big and small schools.

www.usnews.com—The *U.S. News and World Report* publishes the America's Best College guide where you will see more than 1,900 colleges ranked and reviewed.

www.hacu.net—The Hispanic Association of Colleges and Universities web site where you can find information about Hispanic Serving Institutions.

www.princetonreview.com—Great articles on the topic and programs to help you find a good school match.

www.kaplan.edu—Kaplan University.

www.capella.edu—Capella University.

www.university.phoenix.edu—University of Phoenix.

www.devry.edu—Devry University.

www.strayer.edu—Strayer University.

www.wiche.edu—Western Interstate Commission for Higher Education (WICHE). Undergraduate exchange program for students living in one of the WICHE's states and studying out of state. Students may enroll in participating two and four-year institutions and get reduced tuition rates. Participating states: Alaska, Arizona, California, Colorado, Hawaii, Idaho, Montana, Nevada, New Mexico, North Dakota, Oregon, South Dakota, Utah, Washington, and Wyoming.

www.nebhe.org—New England Board of Higher Education (NEBHE). Students are eligible for a tuition break when they enroll in an approved major that is not offered by the public colleges in their own state. Participating states: Connecticut, Maine, Massachusetts, New Hampshire, Rhode Island, and Vermont.

www.sreb.org—Southern Regional Education Board (SREB). It allows residents from one of 16 SREB states to study a degree program not available in their state. Participating states: Alabama, Arkansas, Delaware, Florida, Georgia, Kentucky, Louisiana, Maryland, Mississippi, North Carolina, Oklahoma, South Carolina, Tennessee, Texas, Virginia, and West Virginia

www.mhec.org—Midwestern Higher Education Compact offers the Midwest Student Exchange Program (MSEP). This multi-state tuition reciprocity program allows students from seven states to attend colleges at another participating state. Participating states: Kansas, Michigan, Minnesota, Missouri, Nebraska, North Dakota and Wisconsin.

Books

Been There, Should've Done That: 995 Tips for Making the Most of College by Suzette Tyler (Porch Press, 2008).

Navigating your Freshman Year: How to Make the Leap to College Life-and Land on Your Feet, Students helping students (Penguin Group, 2005).

The Best 366 Colleges, 2008 edition by Princeton Review.

Colleges that Change Lives: 40 Schools that Will Change the Way you Think About Colleges, by Loren Pope (Penguin Group, 2006).

U.S. News Ultimate College Guide 2008, by Staff of the U.S. News &World Report.

The College Board College Handbook 2008, by The College Board.

Fiske Guide to Colleges 2009, by Eduward B. Fiske.

Four Year College, 2008, by Peterson's.

Complete Book of Colleges, 2008 edition, by Princeton Review.

For more information and a constantly updated list of resources log on to **www.latinosincollege.com**.

Chapter 5

ATTENDING A COMMUNITY COLLEGE OR JUNIOR COLLEGE

Many Latinos who opt for a community or junior college do so because they need to work while in school. For these students, community colleges also offer a large selection of classes and programs available online. This allows you to have a more flexible schedule.

But keep in mind that community colleges are also a great option for your post secondary education if you need to get a degree faster. You can obtain an Associate's degree in two years and get a job right away.

As I mentioned in the previous chapter, community colleges are less expensive than four-year schools and they have an open registration policy so everyone can get in regardless of their grades, background or income level.

Although there are many reasons for you to choose a community college, one good reason is to improve your GPA if you don't have the best academic record. Improving your grades may prepare you to attend a good four-year college.

Expert Words

Dolores M. Fernández, Ph.D., president of Eugenio María de Hostos Community College—CUNY (www.hostos.cuny.edu), explains very clearly what community colleges offer: "They offer a multitude of opportunities given the diversity of course offerings and degree options from professional programs in the allied sciences (RN, LPN, Radiology Technician, Dental Hygienist), business, technology to liberal arts. Students just need to inform the counselors of their dreams and community colleges are 'dream catchers' that make those dreams come true." In addition, Dr. Fernández comments that community colleges are the 'workforce development' arm of corporate America. "They have the inside track as to what the current job market requires of their employees and with that information they develop programs that lead to certification in a multitude of areas. These certifications are driven by the market demand."

It's important for you to know that most community colleges have agreements with four-year institutions so that you may transfer after you obtain your Associate's degree. "Usually, the Liberal Arts students are the ones who transfer to a four-year institution upon graduation. Most community colleges have strong articulation agreements with four-year institutions within their immediate geographic area and/or within the system where they are housed. These articulation agreements mean that the receiving schools accept all of the credits from the community college, thereby placing the entering student at a junior level within that four-year receiving institution. If this is the intent of a student entering a community college, he/she must share it with a counselor as soon as possible so that a plan can be developed that will guide the student with course selection," explains Dr. Fernández from Eugenio María de Hostos Community College.

Popular Programs Offered at Community Colleges

These are some of the programs most commonly offered at Community Colleges. There are many more options available, so check your local college to find out what they offer:

- ✓ Business, management, marketing and related support services (business operations support, business administration, accounting, merchandising, hospital administration, etc.)

- ✓ Health professions and related clinical sciences (nursing, allied health diagnostic, health and medical administrative services, dental support services, etc.)

- ✓ Computer and information sciences and support services (computer programming, computer systems networking and telecommunications, data processing, software and media applications, etc.)

- ✓ Liberal arts and sciences, general studies

- ✓ Engineering technologies (drafting/design engineering, electrical engineering technologies, industrial production technicians, mechanical engineering, environmental control, computer engineering, etc.)

✓ Security and protective services (criminal justice and corrections, fire protection, etc.)

✓ Mechanic and repair technologies (vehicle maintenance and repair, electrical/electronics maintenance, heating, air conditioning, ventilation, etc.)

✓ Family and consumer sciences (human development, family studies, foods, nutrition, apparel and textiles, etc.)

Planning To Transfer To a Four-Year School

If your intention is to start your college experience at a community college and transfer to a four-year school, make sure to plan ahead so you don't run into surprises when you're half-way done with your studies.

So, how do you plan ahead? Here are some things you should do:

• Keep your grades up because admission to four-year colleges is competitive.

• Talk to your counselor to determine admission and general education requirements that relate to your transfer.

• Ask about the academic success record the four-year college requires of transfer students.

• Find out about how far in advance you need to apply for a transfer.

• Attend transfer fairs.

• Verify that you can transfer your financial aid.

• Take classes that satisfy the prerequisites and recommended courses for your degree.

To find out more information on transfers, visit the SallieMae website: www.collegeanswer.com

Leveraging The Fact That You Are a Local Resident In Order To Get a Job

Raquel Roque, the owner of Downtown Book Center in Miami, is a great advocate of community colleges. She started her studies at a suburban community college near her home in Miami and switched to Miami Dade Community College when it opened a new campus in downtown Miami. She says: "I attended Miami Dade Community College for two years and then went to Florida International University and majored in Hospitality. People tend to put down community colleges but they offer a great way to get your education. So you can start there and later on you can get your college degree and master's somewhere else. I think that for many Latinos, being in an urban setting helps because they find people who are on the same boat having to work and study. So they understand what you go through and that you can't meet to study in a group all the time."

Raquel's comments are true and they reflect two additional advantages that community colleges offer besides being less expensive than four-year schools: You can find one near your home and, there are many community colleges in urban areas.

Quoting Woody Allen, Raquel Roque, says:
*" 'Eighty percent of success is actually showing up'. Many people
get discouraged because they don't do well in school.
Show up for class and for tutoring. Even if you don't know
what you want to do, just do it. Just show up. The security that
that piece of paper (your degree) gives you is priceless."*

If you have to work while in college, use the fact that you are a local resident to your advantage when looking for a job.

Employers appreciate employees who live in the area because they tend to be more reliable: The shorter the commute, the less chances for someone to be late or absent. So, if you study locally, look for a job that values your skills, offers you a career path within your area of interest, and takes advantage of the fact that you are a member of the community.

Nowadays, most companies do a great deal of community outreach. They support local programs that benefit the community where they do business. So, having employees who have close ties in the area is important to them. As an employee you can get involved in special events such as fund raisers, golf outings, luncheons, little league games, boys/girls scouts, etc. to help create awareness of the company's products and services. The fact that you know the community can help the company develop strategies and improve communication with prospective clients.

When you explore companies that have local branches in your area, look at the kind of programs they support and the types of events they organize. Then try to connect your volunteer experience, both in high school and now, with the work the company does. One thing you may be able to do is help them expand their efforts within the Latino community, for example. Remember this is a segment of the population that companies are eager to reach out to, and thus your knowledge of the Latino community is a major plus for a prospective employer. Something as simple as your ethnic origin can be a great asset, so learn to leverage everything you've got!

Expert Words

Arturo Poiré, the senior human resources expert, shares his view on candidates who start off their education in community colleges and then transfer to a four-year school. "There is no negative reflection on the candidate. Again, the important thing is to have the degree (doesn't matter where you start, even if you start with an Associate's Degree). Personally, I think community colleges are one of the best things of the American education system and I hope the model gets copied to other countries (this is already happening, by the way). There are many reasons why people start their education in community colleges. One of them is if you immigrated into this country, it gives you the opportunity to catch-up in terms of understanding the system, etc. Additionally, they are quite flexible to accept credits from other institutions, even from other countries."

Community colleges are a wonderful destination for the right candidate. They have the flexibility to offer current, up-to-date programs highly valued by employers and some of them are even starting to expand into four-year programs in areas like nursing, technology management, information technology and teaching, to keep up with the demand for these types of occupations.

Once again, make sure that you take a good look at the pros and cons of attending one of these institutions before you enroll, so that you do it because it's in your best interest and not because it's the only way you think you can afford a college education.

WORDS OF ENCOURAGEMENT

Luz Canino-Baker, the managing director of programs and marketing at HACE, shares:

*"Every time I applied for jobs internally
in the bank where I worked the same thing came up:
'Luz, you don't have a degree'. Even when I was a quarter
away from getting my degree, I still didn't get a desired job
because I didn't have a degree. I never have to hear
those words again. I am now in the same game as people
with a degree, so I have a fighting chance."*

CHAPTER RESOURCES

www.collegeanswer.com—The Sallie Mae website dedicated to preparing students for college. It gives information about preparing, selecting, applying and financing your studies.

www.communitycollegetimes.com—The Community College Times is an e-zine dedicated to news and information around community colleges. You will find lots of interesting articles to expand your understanding of community colleges.

www.aacc.nche.edu—The American Association of Community Colleges represents and advocates for more than 1,200 associate-degree granting institutions enrolling more than 12 million students. Here you will find a community college near you as well as statistics and resources.

Books

The Community College Experience: Plus, by Amy Baldwin (Paperback, 2005).

Community College Experience Brief Edition, 2nd by Amy Baldwin (Paperback, 2008).

Community College, Is It Right For You?, by Susan Stafford (Wiley, 2006).

For more information and a constantly updated list of resources log on to **www.latinosincollege.com**.

Chapter 6

LIVING AWAY FROM HOME

If you are currently attending college away from home or if you are considering doing so, it's important for you to learn how to manage a lot more than doing your own laundry or cooking your own meals. Coming from a tight-knit family where your cousins are like your siblings and you consider your aunts and uncles not just your blood relatives but your parents' closest friends as well, it's not easy to live far away. So naturally, you will feel sad when you can't make it home for your birthday or for some important event. Yet, that is by no means reason enough for you to quit school.

Most students, regardless of their cultural or ethnic background experience some level of homesickness, which is to be expected given that it's the first time they live on their own. While it can be exciting to leave home for the first time, it can also be a source of anguish and loneliness, and the secret is to acknowledge these feelings instead of trying to hide them.

WORDS OF ENCOURAGEMENT

María Cecilia Mosquera, an instructor in Clinical Pediatrics at Columbia University/Morgan Stanley Children's Hospital of New York-Presbyterian, shares her experience living on campus after she commuted to school the first couple of years.

"It was much nicer in that I didn't have to commute, I could participate in activities at Loyola (Loyola University New Orleans), I could hang out with friends more, I could join study groups that studied late. College can be challenging but I look back at my memories of friends, interesting classes and college events very fondly. Remember to enjoy it!"

Living on your own and adapting to an entirely different environment can be hard but it can also be a wonderful opportunity for you to become stronger and independent, two valuable traits for your future. So, what can you do to avoid succumbing to the blues?

A Few Tips to Fight Homesickness

Stay in touch

- Getting a good phone plan is crucial when you are away from home because it gives you the freedom to call your family and friends back home without worrying too much about the cost of your phone bill.

- If your parents aren't tech savvy, teach them e-mail basics so you can correspond frequently. If they don't have a computer, they can access one at the local library. E-mailing often will help you feel that you are up to date with family news. On the other hand, you can send pictures and videos of yourself to keep them up to date with your life and activities.

- If you and your parents have an Internet connection and a headset, using Skype (www.Skype.com) will allow you to call each other for free. If you have a camera on your computer, you can even see each other via a video connection! The possibility of seeing one another, even if it's through a computer screen, offers a wonderful chance to connect.

Plan Trips Back Home

Here are some ways to make that happen:

- Try to look for a part time job that gives you enough money to return home a couple of times a year.

- If your parents can afford it, have them visit you on campus. This way they get a chance to share in your life and they don't feel excluded from it. Keep in mind that if they haven't attended college themselves, the whole experience may be foreign to them. You might want to tell them all about it ahead of time, so that they don't feel awkward or out of place.

- If you have friends in college who are from your hometown (or near enough) you may want to consider sharing rides during your trips back home for holidays and school breaks. This will help reduce the travel cost and it will give you time to rest from driving, which makes the journey safer.

- Most colleges have a "ride board". It posts where students will be driving and how to buy a spot in their car. Students share the cost of gas and get a ride home for very little money. This can be a great option as well.

Be mindful, however, that you should try to balance staying in touch with your family with becoming an independent person. For this to happen, you will need to avoid using your family as a crutch in this new stage of your life. Talk to them, email them and visit them but remember than in order to adapt to your new life away from home, you also need to learn to be comfortable with some distance between you and your family. And the distance is not only geographical. Your college years are a unique opportunity to begin seeing your life as your own, and marking your independence (both geographically and emotionally) is an important step in taking the reins of your future.

WORDS OF ENCOURAGEMENT

Regardless of your interests in school and in life,
nothing will help you achieve more than aiming for your best.
Marisela Riveros, the senior TV producer tells you where
she got her inspiration from:

"My dad, who passed away, always told me:
'No matter what career you choose, you have to be the best at it.'

He said that to me every day in regards to all the different classes
I took: Tae kwon do, swimming and tennis. He wanted me
to be the best at everything I did, and he continued to
tell me the same thing when I started college."

Home for the Holidays

You may have been dreaming about going back home for weeks or months when the day finally arrives and you realize it is not going as you planned. Many things have changed. For starters, you have gotten used to living on your own, not reporting to your parents or asking for permission to do everything you do. You have become more independent and it may not be easy for them to deal with that when you are back amongst them, sleeping in your old room, playing or hanging out with your younger siblings.

Most likely, you will need to have a polite conversation with your family where you re-establish the rules you will live by when you are home. For example: "Mom, Dad, Grandma, I'm so glad to be home. I missed you guys so much! Can we agree on the fact that I'm a little more independent now and maybe I don't need to ask you for permission to stay up late? And if I tell you who I'm going to be with and where, will it be okay for me not to have a curfew?"

This is just an example to give you a general idea of how to approach the subject. Start by telling them how much you love them and miss them while in school. Be as specific as possible about what you missed. Whether it was your mom's cooking or going with the family to church on Sundays or anything else. (Be prepared to put your money where you mouth is, though. So, if you say you missed going to mass on Sundays, you better be ready to get up early that Sunday to join your family in prayer!)

After you spend some time talking about this, bring up the fact that you've gotten used to living on your own and need a "little" more independence now. Don't ask for too much at once, you know how Latino parents and grandparents feel about their kids. You'll always be a baby for them!

Going home will bring back lots of warm feelings. Being surrounded by your loving family will give you that sense of belonging that perhaps you don't feel is completely there yet at school. As much as we all crave for that fantastic feeling, don't give into the temptation of deciding to stay home because you feel better than at school. There will be many situations in your life when you will have to overcome certain level of discomfort, and practicing overcoming that discomfort is the best you can do for your future. Work on finding your place in school rather than opting to stay home because "fitting in at school" is too hard. It will get better every day. Remember: Anything worth its while is worth fighting for.

Develop a Support System

Having a strong support system at school is a good way to fend off the blues and develop a sense of belonging. Your friends are the first obvious place to go when you are feeling a little down. Most likely, you are not the only one who gets sad once in a while, and talking to people who can relate to your feelings will immediately make you feel better.

But friends are not the only ones who can help you here. Another great source of support is your Resident Advisor (RA). RAs are undergraduate students who have gone through a special training to assist residents within the halls. (A great job to put on your resumé and a wonderful way to save money in tuition, housing and meals, by the way!) Their responsibilities include: Helping to develop a sense of community in the hall through social events, educational opportunities and other activities; acting as peer counselors, assisting professional staff in crisis situations and others. They are closer to your age than your professors and they may very well experience (or have experienced) the same homesickness you do but they may know how to handle it better. So, if you're feeling a little down, talk to your RA and ask him/her how he/she deals with this emotion.

If you notice that your sadness is not temporary, and that you have a hard time concentrating, waking up, or sleeping, that your body aches and you have no interest in things that normally interest you, you may be depressed. If this is the case, it's important that you make an appointment with a psychiatrist on campus so you can receive the appropriate help. The important thing is that you remember that there is no shame in looking for help (something with which you may have grown up, given the stigma that the Latino community places on therapy). Not only are you not the only one to face difficulties at school, but on top of if there are plenty of people on campus who are there to help you. Don't be afraid to reach out.

WORDS OF ENCOURAGEMENT

Maira Mercado, scholarship recipient and
college student attending Claremont McKenna College,
in Claremont, California, who won one of the four
RMHC/HACER $100,000 national scholarships, suggests:

*"I believe that you should be positive, stay balanced, work hard,
and have a plan. Believe in yourself, take challenges, try new
things, and look at the night sky; there are so many stars,
so many things to discover, so many great things to do.
And most importantly, enjoy the adventure!"*

Engage in Interesting Activities

Don't underestimate the power of engaging in activities that interest you. I know at times it may be a "chicken or the egg" situation where you don't have the desire to do anything but doing something will definitely make you feel better. So, make an effort to go listen to an interesting guest speaker or to join the drama club or the basketball team. Becoming involved with people and activities that intrigue you will take your mind off your homesickness and it will help you focus your energy in the present.

Learn to Breathe Through Your Stomach

Yes, I know you don't see the connection between breathing and overcoming your homesickness but think about it this way: One of the effects of focusing your breathing in your stomach (versus breathing through your chest) is that it reduces your anxiety and it brings you out of your head and into the present. So, whenever you feel sad, or anxious or angry this little exercise will help you relax and calm down.

Lie down on your back or sit up straight and breathe slowly through your stomach. That means, inhale counting to five while filling up your belly like a big balloon. Hold for a count of five and let the air out slowly through your nose for a count of five. Repeat this several times until you feel that all the tension, fear, anxiety or sadness has been released.

Try to continue breathing through your stomach during the day so that you remain in the present. By focusing on what's happening here and now, instead of how much you miss your bed, your mom's spaghetti or your uncle Ramon's jokes, you'll focus on the game you are watching with your friends or the book you are reading right now for your English lit class or the conversation you are having with your roommate.

WORDS OF ENCOURAGEMENT

"If you are not having an exciting experience in college, change something you are doing: Change your major, get involved with a study group . . . do something that excites you and you will be on your way. I spoke no Chinese when I went for a month to China on a special program and I was blown away by the experience. It changed my life in such a way that I started taking language courses and I now speak Mandarin Chinese," shares James Kopelman, Associate Producer at After Ed.TV at Teacher's College, Columbia University, who attended the University of Oklahoma on a National Merit Scholarship and graduated Magna Cum Laude.

Latinos in College

Change your Thoughts

The only way to make yourself sad, angry, anxious or successful and happy is through your thoughts. People who think they can win a game, use this positive belief to propel them to give the best they have to win the game. These people will usually succeed at whatever they undertake. They focus on their goal, they train hard and they keep their belief that they will win the game.

Now, people who always think that they will do badly on a test and that they will fail because they are good for nothing, will feel nervous before the test and most likely will fail it. Some people call this a "self-fulfilling prophecy."

The secret is that by changing your thoughts you can change your feelings. Granted, this is not easy to do, but it is definitely possible because you can train your brain like you train a muscle. Let's look at some common thoughts and how you could turn them around for a positive impact.

Negative thought	Change it to
"I don' fit in here."	"I'm learning the culture of this school so I can flourish."
"I miss my parents, I want to go home."	"I miss my parents, it will be great to see them for Christmas."
"I hate making changes."	"I've made changes before and I learned a lot from them."
"I'm too anxious, I can't concentrate."	"I'm learning to relax to achieve top concentration."
"I'm different from them, they don't like me."	"We are all unique people and I have a lot to offer."

You can be experiencing any number of thoughts that may be the culprits of you feeling sad, homesick, anxious, etc. Learn to analyze your thoughts so you can change them. The best way to accomplish this is by catching yourself when you experience one of these feelings. For instance, let's say you feel sad. Stop whatever you are doing and ask yourself: "Why am I sad?" "What's making me feel this way?" "What am I thinking about at this very moment that is making me feel sad?" Say that after some soul-searching you come up with an answer like: "I was thinking about my sister and the day she and I went to the movies together and laughed hysterically. I miss her!" So that's when you redirect your thoughts into: "I'm going to talk to my friend Janet and tell her about my sister. That will make me feel good." Or "I'm going to call my sister and tell her I miss her and tell her all the things I'm doing here and how exciting life in campus is."

Noticing what thoughts make you upset is the first step to changing the way you feel. The same is true regarding thoughts about yourself. If you often feel unworthy, or that you don't belong, or that you are not good enough, good-looking enough, smart enough, etc., you may need to shift your thoughts about yourself. Again, detect what you are thinking at the moment the bad feeling arises and change that thought. For instance if you often think: "I'm not smart enough for this school" change it to: "I'm smart and I will learn whatever I don't know from books and from the people around me." You get the idea.

CHAPTER RESOURCES

www.skype.com—If you and your parents have Internet access, you can download this program to talk over the Internet for free.

www.susankramer.com/TeenMeditation.html—This website gives you lots of meditation exercises which can help you overcome your homesickness and also achieve better concentration.

www.wildmind.org/—This Buddhist meditation site allows you to teach yourself how to mediate, read about meditation, and find others for support. You will find guides to posture, learn about mantra meditation, mindful breathing, walking meditation and applied meditation for stress management for example.

www.campusblues.com—A wonderful site to find lots of articles about overcoming homesickness, mental health, drugs, alcohol and sex, healthy eating habits and a lot more related to your college life.

Books

Get Out of Your Mind and Into Your Life: The New Acceptance and Commitment Therapy, by Steven C. Hayes.

Your Mind: The Owner's Manual, by Linda Joy Rose, Ph.D.

Meditation for Dummies by Stephan Bodian and Dean Ornish.

For more information and a constantly updated list of resources log on to **www.latinosincollege.com**.

Chapter 7

CHOOSING COURSES AND DECLARING YOUR MAJOR

What Is a Major?

One of the peculiarities of four-year colleges in America is the fact that, at some point during your studies, you need to choose a major: An organized group of classes connected to a subject, a theme or a professional field. You can major in English (subject), Business sustainability (theme) or Engineering (professional field). It's important to notice that not all colleges have majors but those that do, have them in order for you to have a structured curriculum before you graduate and also, to set a minimum academic standard for your work.

This is quite different from the university system in most of Latin America where you spend an average of five years studying for one particular career and you graduate with the equivalent of a Master's degree. This means that you have to decide what you want to be when you grow up by the time you are a senior in high school. For example, if you want to be an accountant, you study accounting for five years; if you want to be an architect, you study architecture for five years. The advantage of the American system is that you can study all sorts of things before you have to decide your specialty (major), and even then, you don't always need to choose your major in the same field as your Master's degree.

Choosing your major is a big decision, as it will impact what courses you take, but it's one that you can change, if you find that you made the wrong choice. If you decide what you want to do early on, however, you may fulfill the course requirements and graduate on time, and you may also gain access to many internships that are major-dependent (See Chapter 7).

Although choosing a major is definitely important, my suggestion is that you don't worry excessively about making the *right* choice. What's important right now is that you follow your interests and passions and that you realize that your major is not necessarily connected to your future career. Leylha Ahuile's story is a perfect example: "I changed my major five times: business, political science, psychology, sociology and oceanography. I ended up studying business with a minor in political science, but as I kept changing my major, I took classes that broaden my view on topics I wouldn't have been exposed to had I stuck with one major. All of this knowledge is what allows me to do different things right now. To me, college teaches you how to be a student for life," says Ms. Ahuile, the founder of Tinta Fresca (www.tintafresca.us), an online Spanish-language book review website.

Time to Choose

Even though most schools require that you look at your major by your sophomore year, there are some that require you to list your choice on your application. If you haven't decided what you'd like to study at the time you're submitting your application, just check "undecided." Now keep in mind that some majors require a large number of courses, therefore if this is the case of the major you are considering, you may need to declare it early in order to fulfill the course and graduate on time.

Some majors require that you take prerequisite courses and this is where changing majors may cost you additional time if you have to take new prerequisites for your new major. Check your college's latest catalog or your school's website to find out the guidelines for the different majors.

WORDS OF ENCOURAGEMENT

*"I think that education is the great equalizer in society.
We couldn't choose the grammar school and the high school we
attended, those decisions belonged to our parents.
But, college is the first real choice in life we make, so choose
it wisely. Try to figure out what your passion is early on,
so that you choose the right major and stick to it, no matter
what others say. While in school, build your own social network,
keeping in mind that these students will be running corporations
and organizations in the future so you want to maintain
contact with them even after you graduate. Once you have
solid credentials, as you apply for jobs you will be better able to
sell yourself and compete on an equal playing field."*

—Luz Canino-Baker, Managing Director
Programs/Marketing at HACE

Common Mistakes

When it comes to choosing courses and declaring a major, people have all sorts of misconceptions. Let's make sure we review the most important ones so you are well equipped to make your decisions.

MYTH: Getting your general education courses out of the way before you even think about a major is a good idea.

FACT: The truth is that this is not really such a good idea because:
- There are some courses that count for certain majors but not for others.
- Usually, you can't use courses from your own major to meet the general education requirements. For example, if you major in history, you can't use any of the history courses to meet your social science requirements.

    A better option is to talk to your advisor and carefully choose your general education requirements.

MYTH: To find about a major, the best you can do is to take courses in it.

FACT: Not such a good idea! You will only eliminate one major at a time.
- Many introductory courses are not a good example of what the major will be like.
- Sometimes colleges won't let you take major courses until you are enrolled in the major.

A much better idea is to read through the course description, to sit in a few classes to see if the major interests you and again, to talk to your advisor.

MYTH: Selecting a major is the same thing as choosing your career.

FACT: This is not really true. People who major in philosophy, for instance, are seen as good thinkers and can go into many different fields, from human resources, to business as in Andrea Sáenz's case. "When I chose my major, I wasn't thinking about college in terms of career prep. I decided to study what I found exciting and interesting, which at the time was philosophy, history and literature. I ended up with a self-designed major in Latin American Studies, which was great while in school and would have been wonderful had I elected an academic career. I didn't apply my college major to my career. Instead, I enjoyed college for the pure joy of learning about the world, improving my writing skills and meeting interesting people. I then pursued a graduate degree to support my career interests," says Andrea Sáenz, president of Hispanic Alliance for Career Enhancement

Many schools offer double majors and others give you the chance of choosing a major and a minor which can be completed without extra time. Also, keep in mind that you could follow Ms. Sáenz' example and choose a major for your undergraduate degree and a different one for your Master's degree. Maybe you should even consider leaving your career major for your Master's degree so that you give yourself the opportunity to learn other things before you delve into your career fully.

WORDS OF ENCOURAGEMENT

David Peña, Jr., the executive director of National Hispanic Business Association, comments: *"Looking back I now feel that the best part of going to college was the doors of opportunity that an education has given me. In addition, I have been able to*

break the generational cycle of being a farm worker and now
being a professional who can help his family."

Your Family's Input On Your
Major and Your Career

If your family is anything like mine, they will most likely try to "guide" you towards what you should study. Sometimes, in Latino families, men get more pressure than women regarding their career choices and this was the case in my house. My brother had to study medicine whereas, as long as we went to college, my sister and I could choose whatever we wished. Granted, many years have passed since I went to college, but the reality is that a lot of that still goes on today.

In addition, many parents who encourage their children to go to college still have some preconceptions regarding certain careers. I often hear parents say things like "Engineering is not a career for a woman," or "No man should study literature." These two statements couldn't be farther from the truth. There are incredible opportunities in Engineering for both women and men in this country and in the world. As a matter of fact, the demand for engineers is such that there aren't enough professionals to cover all the positions available now and in the future.

Regarding this issue, Henry Lescaille, Executive Director, of Human Resources, at Time Inc. shares his perspective: "My parents (neither having had the opportunity to attend college) were incredibly supportive of my academic goals. Their main objective and desire was that I would find work that was both fulfilling personally but also financially rewarding. They strongly encouraged a career in Law (which I entertained).

However, after working at a law firm for a summer, I realized that while I might have the mental agility for law, my heart was simply not in it. They were supportive—and I feel that you can always glean wisdom from parents—so I would listen to their feedback and thoughts."

So, whether your family is pushing you to either follow a career path you don't want to follow or to not follow the one you want, here are my suggestions:

- Find statistics on women and men in your field of study and share them with your family.

- Find examples of successful professionals in the career you wish to pursue and share them.

- Ask your advisor to help you put together a list of professions you could pursue with your major and show it to your parents.

- Talk to your parents about the opportunities available for people in the field of your interest. To find out the projected growth of each occupation and profession, visit: www.bls.gov/oco and check out the Occupational Outlook Handbook, a directory published by the government.

- If your parents were born overseas or if they were born here but didn't graduate from college, share with them the number of options open to students in this country regardless of their gender. Also tell them that allowing you to study what you feel passionate about will put you on the path to success. You will always be better at doing something you are passionate about.

When talking to your parents about this issue, try to be open and patient and most of all, try to understand their position: They love you and they want what is best for you. They've done a great job raising you, so always listen to their advice before you make a decision. In the end, it is your future and it is your decision to make even if at times you feel a little conflicted.

WORDS OF ENCOURAGEMENT

*"I always felt that if I studied political science
I'd have to work on that for the rest of my life. I was made
to feel that if I took classes in Psychology or Sociology
I was wasting my time. There is no one class that I took that
was a waste of time. While you are in school, as long as you
study, you're making good use of your time. You have to study
what you are passionate about. The most successful
CEO and smartest person I ever met (and for whom I worked)
once told me: 'Study what you love and everything else
will follow.' He had a Bachelor's of Art in History and was
extremely successful,"* says Leylha Ahuile, founder of
Tinta Fresca, an online Spanish book review website.

CHAPTER RESOURCES

www.bls.gov/oco—The Occupational Outlook Handbook is a directory published by the federal government where you can find every single occupation in this country along with a description of the educational requirements, what the job entails, the average salary and growth projection.

www.collegeboard.com/student/csearch/majors_careers/468.html— Great article on declaring your major on The College Board's website.

Books

What Color Is Your Parachute For Teens: Discovering Yourself, Defining Your Future, by Richard Nelson Bolles, Carol Christen and Jean M. Blomquist (Ten Speed Press, 2006).

Teen's Guide to College and Career Success: Your High School Roadmap for College and Career Success. (Peterson's, 2008).

How to Choose a College Major, revised and updated edition by Linda Landis Andrews (McGraw Hill Companies, 2006).

For more information and a constantly updated list of resources log on to **www.latinosincollege.com**.

Chapter 8

SHOW ME THE DOUGH! SCHOLARSHIPS BEYOND FRESHMAN YEAR

If you are still in high school, you should know that there are billions of dollars in scholarships out there to help you pay for school. There are scholarships for all sorts of students (not just A students), for an incredible range of interests, for people who are members of certain organizations, or that belong to certain religions. It's hard to describe the huge diversity of scholarships available so, if you haven't done so yet, become familiar with the scholarship search engines I'm including at the end of this chapter.

One very important place to look is the Hispanic Scholarship Fund's website (www.hsf.net). Not only do they offer many scholarships but, in addition, they manage the Gates Millennium Scholars Program (GMS) that can provide funding for your entire education up to 10 years! You have to be a first time freshman but the scholarship is available for

non-traditional students as well. So, if you have a GED or if you graduated from high school a few years ago and you are only now thinking
about applying to college you could apply. You have to be eligible for Federal Aid and the Pell grant and you have to submit your FAFSA. "The
scholarship covers up to need," explains Cathy Makunga, Sr. Director for
Scholarship Programs at the Hispanic Scholarship Fund. "Using the student's financial aid award letter and GMS awarding policies, the GMS
scholarship funds a student's unmet need based on their cost of atten-
dance including tuition, room, board, books, meals and fees . . . That
means within their financial aid, it covers anything the student normally
has to cover out of pocket and is individualized to the student's need."

Advice from a Scholarship Winner

Brian Campos, entering freshman at Harvard University—class of
2012—is one of the four winners of the $100,000 national Ronald
McDonald House Charities/HACER scholarship (www.meencanta.com).
Here he shares his thoughts on how to get scholarships: "I think the most
important factor is to maintain high grades, to obtain leadership positions and to look for internships not only in one field but in several areas
because you never know what you could be interested in. I come from a
poor economic situation, living with my single mother and sister, and
usually, in situations like mine, resources are so scarce that it's hard to
accomplish anything. But I didn't let that get me down; I was passionate
about learning and I had the support of those around me. I excelled academically ever since elementary school and that granted me the chance
to take exams to get into Hunter College High School (one of the top
high schools in the nation) and to get into Prep for Prep (a highly selec-

tive program as well). I stood out at both institutions and more opportunities presented themselves, allowing me to gain the knowledge and experience that I now have. Hunter, apart from giving me a top-notch education, gave me the chance to take leadership roles and to intern at a prestigious sports magazine. Prep for Prep, an organization that helps out gifted minority students from the New York City area, encouraged me to explore various industries and to encounter different types of people and ideas by traveling abroad. It's all about being open to what's out there and looking for any opportunities that come your way. If they don't, then take initiative and search for them."

I want you to get in the habit of thinking that there is a lot of money out there to help you pay for college even once you are in college. Don't pay attention to those who tell you that you won't be able to afford school and please, I will say it once again, don't just choose a school based on how much you can pay. Rather choose it based on how wonderfully it matches your goals and your personality.

Looking for money to pay for your tuition, books, and room and board should be considered a year-round activity. Martin Curiel, founder of Rising Farmworker Dream Fund (www.risingfarmwork ers.org), who got an average of $15,000 a year in scholarships and got out of school debt free (graduated with an Engineering degree from California Polytechnic), came up with a great way to think about this issue.

"I did the math," he explains. "I put in an average of four hours per scholarship application and I applied to about 25 scholarships a year that were between $500 and $1,000. Of those, I got an average of 18 which means I invested 100 hours to get about $15,000. That means I made $150 an hour. My question was: "How many hours do I need to work at $10 an hour (which is what students get) to come up with $15,000?" Many students use the lack of time as an excuse for not applying for scholarships when the truth is that they are wasting more time working at $10 an hour. Money was never an issue for me because I had more scholarship money than I needed."

Nara Alvarez, a junior at University of San Diego, wishes she had known earlier in her career how easy it was to apply for scholarships. "I only found out when I was a sophomore because my younger sister, who at the time was in high school, applied and got lots of money that way. So, I decided to try." She now has a system all set up. "I spend about 10-13 hours a week researching, and because I've been doing it for a while, I have lots of resources. Then I spend around 10 hours a month filling out applications. All in all I apply to 50 to 100 scholarships a year and get around 40 percent of them." Just as Martin Curiel, Nara applies to smaller scholarships of between $500 and $1,000 but what's interesting about her is that she also applies when she doesn't qualify, and guess what? She gets the scholarships anyway!

If You Don't Qualify, Apply Anyway!

Nara Alvarez, a junior at University of San Diego, received scholarships even when she didn't qualify for them. Here are a few examples:

- "I applied to a scholarship for Latino students majoring in Finance and living in San Francisco. I live in San Diego but I got it anyway."

- "I applied to a Coca-Cola scholarship for students going into Sales and given that my major was in business I felt I should qualify. I wrote that in my essay and I got the scholarship."

- "Many times scholarships require that students be doing certain things in the present that I may not be doing in the present, but that I did in the past. What I do then, is I explain my past experience in my essay."

- "Also, many scholarships are for students who want to work in the non-profit sector. And, although I want to work in business, my goal in the future, when I'm wealthy, is to have my own non-profit organization so I can contribute to the community. By aligning my goals with their goals, I usually get the scholarship."

Applying to scholarships is very important but making sure you have what it takes to get a scholarship is as critical. Cathy Makunga, Sr. Director for Scholarship Programs at HSF, says regarding the Gates Millennium Scholars scholarship: "We are not just looking at the GPA. We want to see if they show leadership qualities, if they are using support networks; if they are looking at the future, if they have goals in mind. Are they being realistic? If their goal is to be a doctor, have they taken any science courses? When the readers look at a scholarship application, they look at the opportunities offered at that particular high school and then they see if the student took advantage of them. So, if the school offers ten AP courses, and the student took only one, they wonder why. We are also looking for students that are involved in their community, are change agents and leaders."

Scholarships for Sophomores, Juniors and Seniors

Many scholarships that you receive can be renewed year after year—and the reapplication process is easier because you've already filled out the forms once—but many students forget to reapply or can't reapply because they haven't kept up with the requirements: They let their GPAs, change schools, change majors, etc. So, watch out for these changes if you wish to reapply to a scholarship with strict requirements. Remember to read the fine print to make sure you are still eligible if your situation has recently changed.

There are many scholarships available for second, third and fourth year students. As a matter of fact, once you declare your major, a lot of new opportunities for scholarships open up. Corporations that are looking for students who are interested in their industries offer both scholarships and internships and sometimes a combination of both. So, for instance, if you are a nursing major in your junior or senior year of school, you could apply to a scholarship offered by Kaiser Permanente.

At this stage of the game, you should also explore scholarships offered by professional organizations that are related to your field of study. For example, the Hispanic College Fund (www.hispanicfund.org) in partnership with the Association of Latino Professionals in Finance and Accounting—ALPFA—(www.alpfa.org) offers a scholarship for undergraduate and graduate students pursuing studies in Accounting, Finance, IT or related fields.

Ana Esquivel, executive director, Corporate Internship Program and Student Services at the Hispanic Association of Colleges and Universities—HACU—(www.hacu.net) says: "For the 2008-2009 period we are awarding $350,000 in scholarships sponsored by our partner-corporations. They are usually major-specific, like GM's scholarship is for engineering majors, and for some of them, students can reapply every year as long as funds are available."

Now, given that scholarships have different deadlines, it's important that you do your research year round to find funding sources and that you put them on a calendar so you can apply early and not miss any of them.

Every year you should apply for scholarships to pay for your next year of school and it will be easier if you simply add this activity to your schedule, as if it were part of your course load. Think about the positive side of doing this extra work: You won't be in debt when you graduate!

Words from a Scholarship Winner

Gregorio Hallman Jr., the doctoral student at Teacher's College, Columbia University, has paid his entire college education (undergraduate, graduate and now doctorate) with the Gates Millennium Scholars Program. "Over time I must have gotten $300,000 in funding. I wasn't the smartest or the strongest or the fastest student. This scholarship is all about leadership and I got it because I was involved. So, instead of going to the mall or playing sports, I volunteered. I showed up and helped people. I know a lot of Latinos who received this scholarship."

Tips To Be More Successful at Finding Scholarships

• Learn how to write powerful essays and have someone with a great command of English grammar review them for you. There are websites on the Internet (www.essayinfo.com; www.scholarship.com) where you can learn how to write essays and you can read successful pieces. You can also take writing courses.

• If you have to include letters of recommendation with your application, make sure that they don't contradict your essay in any way. For instance, if in your essay you say that you volunteered 200 hours, make sure the person recommending you doesn't write that you volunteered only 150.

• Even when you use basically the same essay for several scholarship applications, make sure that you adapt it for each particular situation. Readers can tell when you make the extra effort to customize your essay to their application.

• Dedicate a few hours a week during the entire year, to search for scholarships and fill out applications.

• Don't just look on the Internet. Visit your school library, ask your counselors, your professors, upper classmen and anyone you know for information on scholarships. "People want to help," says Martin Curiel. "The moment you show some initiative, people give you leads."

• Visit your financial aid office OFTEN. "If you don't put the effort to get the funds, they won't do anything. Don't expect them to reach out and tell you what's available. You have to persist yourself," says Carla Rivera, a junior at Pace University.

• Use different search engines and websites to look for scholarships as you will get different results. Check out a few interesting ones in the Chapter Resources section at the end of the chapter.

• Apply to scholarships even if you don't fulfill all the requirements. If you have a powerful essay, the person reading it and reviewing your application may decide you're worth giving a scholarship to. Always remember that there are individuals, not abstract institutions, making a decision. Your goal is to impact these individuals.

- Apply to smaller and local scholarships because less people apply to those and your chances of getting them are automatically higher.

- Fill out the entire application form, submit everything you are asked to and send it on time to meet the deadline.

Finally, if you or your parents can't get loans because you don't have a credit history, contact local credit unions and local companies that specialize in working with Latinos. There are many organizations across the country helping minorities build their credit history by lending them money at a decent rate. You'll find a few websites in the Chapter Resources section below.

WORDS OF ENCOURAGEMENT

Brian Campos, the scholarship winner attending Harvard University, shares these words: *"It's all about your smarts and the drive in you to succeed on all levels, not only academically. Of course, my mother's support and her wise words that an education is key to escaping the poverty cycle were also very important to me. I know I'm just starting out and there's so much more to do. I'm excited to face the obstacles ahead and accomplish much more than I already have. Never be afraid to fail. One needs to have a positive attitude in order to overcome adversity and to get far in life."*

CHAPTER RESOURCES

www.ed.gov/programs/fws/index.html—Here is the federally funded work-study program offered by the U.S. Department of Education.

www.ecampustours.com—Follow the links so you can find tips on how to fill out the FAFSA and a checklist of the information you will need to have handy.

www.hsf.net—Hispanic Scholarship Fund is the Hispanic organization that distributes the largest amount of money in scholarships for Latinos.

www.hispanicfund.org—The Hispanic College Fund is a non-profit organization that offers many scholarships for Latinos sponsored by various corporations.

www.scholarshipsforhispanics.com—This website is a great directory of many scholarships for Hispanics available in the market.

www.maldef.org—The Mexican American Legal Defense and Educational Fund offers scholarships for law students but most importantly, in their website you will find a list of scholarships available to students regardless of their immigration status.

www.latinocollegedollars.org—This site features scholarships for Latino students compiled by The Tomás Rivera Policy Institute. You can choose whether you are a high school, college or graduate student, your GPA and if citizenship is required or not and it will give you a list of opportunities. Watch out because some scholarships listed under "citizenship not required" have certain requirements that only documented students can fulfill like: "Must be eligible for federal aid."

www.fastweb.com—This is the search engine of **www.finaid.org** and once you register for free and fill out your profile, it will match you with a long list of possible scholarships.

www.studentscholarshipsearch.com—This website offers a free guide published by Student Loan Network, written by Christopher S. Penn, to help you improve your chances of getting scholarships.

www.college-scholarships.com—Offers a list of scholarships sites for college students in traditional schools and studying online.

www.internationalscholarships.com—In case you want to study abroad, here is a great website to help you find funding for your adventure!

www.petersons.com—This is a very comprehensive resource for you to look for scholarships and financial aid, to get help with your essays and test preparation.

www.hacu.net—The Hispanic Association of Colleges and Universities is a non-profit organization that offers scholarships, helps students find internships and study-abroad opportunities. It also offers great opportunities to network at their annual conference and various events.

www.progressfin.com—Progress Financial, it's a company based in California that lends money to Latinos with limited or no credit history.

www.nclup.org—It's the Network of Latino Credit Unions and Professionals. In their website you will find a number of credit union members based in various areas of the country. Contact the one near you to find out about student loans.

www.hispanicheritage.org—The Hispanic Heritage Foundation (HHF) identifies, inspires, promotes and prepares Latino role models through national leadership, cultural, educational and workforce programs. They offer scholarships and a program called LOFT (Latinos on Fast Track) that can help direct you to great paid internships and job opportunities.

Books

Winning Scholarships for College, An Insider's Guide, by Marianne Ragins (winner of more than $400,000 in scholarship money) (Holt Paperbacks, 2004).

Scholarship Pursuit; The How to Guide for Winning College Scholarships by S.Y. Koot author, Dr. Arthur L.Jue, contributor and Corine Neumiller, contributor. (Paperback, 2008).

Scholarship Handbook 2009 by The College Board.

Scholarship Vault (Your College Cash Connection) by John Pyzik-(Kindle Edition, 2008).

Kaplan Scholarships 2009 Edition: Billions of Dollars in Free Money for College, by Kaplan (Paperback, 2008).

For more information and a constantly updated list of resources log on to **www.latinosincollege.com**.

Chapter 9

JOBS, CO-OPS AND INTERNSHIPS DURING COLLEGE

Many Latino students face a difficult reality: They need to work to pay for their studies or to help their families. David Peña Jr., the Executive Director of the National Hispanic Business Association, comes from a family of farm workers. During his college years Mr. Peña was on a tight schedule of classes, student employment and internships to help pay for school. He shares: "Being away [from home] was financially difficult since I was now attending an urban university where the costs are significantly higher, and I could not depend on my family for any financial assistance. However, being away from home taught me some valuable lessons on budgeting, social networking and goal setting. I learned to survive with the resources and tools I had."

If you can't afford to study full time, it's important that you choose your jobs wisely so that they build your resume and they allow you enough time to study.

But keep in mind that the worse thing that could happen to you right now is that you get derailed and you quit school. Here's something you should be mindful of: Studies show that the completion of your degree highly depends on your enrollment intensity. This means that studying part time doesn't yield the same graduation rate as studying full time, and of course you can imagine why.

There are stories all around you of students who found a great $500 a week job right out of high school and decided to forget about college. Who needs college if you can make money like this without a degree, right? Wrong! Those $500 that sound fantastic today, will not sound so hot in ten years when you are still making the same amount, precisely because you don't have a degree. And $500 may feel like a lot now that you're still living at home and have few expenses. Once you have to pay your own rent, utilities, food, transportation, clothes, or support a child, it won't be enough to live above the poverty level.

So if you do have to work while you are in school, you need to be extra committed to overcome the "temptation" to quit. With a college degree you will be much better equipped to help your family. Don't let a short-term concern take your focus away from the big prize that awaits those who persevere and get a four-year degree.

Statistics to Keep You Focused

- Latinos lag behind every other major population in attaining college degrees, especially bachelor's degrees. (Vernez & Mizell, 2002)

- Latinos are the least likely young college students to be pursuing their studies full time.

- Among undergraduates who enrolled full time at public four-year colleges, 57 percent completed a bachelor's degree, but only 28 percent did if they initially enrolled part time. (NCES, 2002b)

Studying part time has two main consequences:

1. It takes much longer to graduate and you may become frustrated or get discouraged.

2. It will limit your opportunities for socializing with other students and professors, a very important part of the college experience that will impact your future. Luz Canino-Baker, Managing Director Programs/ Marketing at the Hispanic Alliance for Career Enhancement—HACE— (www.hace-usa.org), shares: "As a part time student there was no real social life at school. As for working full time, it took tremendous discipline. There was no time to hang out with friends, no time to read magazines and books I wanted to read." Because Luz got married after her freshman year, she put school on hold until her baby was three years old. She went back to school while she worked full time and raised a family. It took her eight years to complete her undergraduate degree. Now, while it's possible, you can see from Luz's experience that it's definitely not ideal. As fascinating as school can be, who wants to be in college for almost a decade?

WORDS OF ENCOURAGEMENT

*"Students need to persevere and be cognizant
that the path may be bumpy and filled with obstacles but
that they can achieve anything they set their
minds and hearts to achieve."*

—Dolores M. Fernández, President,
Eugenio María de Hostos Community College, CUNY

Jennifer Quintano, a student at Brooklyn College in Brooklyn, New York, majoring in early childhood education shares what it's been like for her to study while working full time: "Due to my family's financial situation I've been working during all my years in school. I work 40 hours a week within the Brooklyn Public Library System. It has affected my studies a great deal in that I was forced to leave school for one year to get settled within the organization. I have also been unable to join clubs or participate in internships due to my full schedule during the day. I attend school part time during the evening session, which provides a limited number of courses at that time. It takes determination and drive to work full time and attend school at night. While I don't recommend it, I can say that is possible from personal experience to do both, especially when your life situation demands it."

Expert Words

Marcia Vargas, VP-US Inclusion and Diversity at McDonald's Corporation, worked part time during the year and full time during the summers all through high school and college. She worked sales in various retail environments and held various positions at a medical facility as admissions officer and financial aid counselor picking up a wide variety of skills that served her well when she graduated. And although it was hard to balance her work and her studies, by the time she was in college she had figured out that she didn't need to get an A in everything but in her major courses. "You need to learn to prioritize because working, family, community and having a 4.0 GPA on everything is just not going to happen. So, I had a 3.0 GPA in everything but a 3.5 in all my major courses."

There is no question about the fact that the best thing you can do is to focus on your studies full time and to try to keep the highest possible GPA. But if your life situation forces you to work, or if you have other family commitments to fulfill, it's interesting to keep in mind Ms. Vargas' advice and to make sure that you work hard at keeping a high GPA in the courses of your major.

Consider Co-op Opportunities

Many colleges offer co-op programs. Although the structure varies from school to school, in many cases it means that you study full time for a semester and work full time for a semester. In general, you co-op for three terms and graduate within five years. You acquire experiential credit for the semester you are on co-op but not academic credit. Both your academic advisor and your co-op coordinator (someone who specializes in your major) work together to coordinate your classroom and co-op experiences.

What is interesting about co-op programs is that they allow you to explore your fields of interest, acquire skills and experience as well as develop contacts that may later lead to full-time job offers as employers like to hire students who are not starting in the field from scratch.

You usually need to declare a major before you can start your co-op. Many universities offer co-ops in cities and states other than where they are located and some offer opportunities abroad. The program usually requires that you stay with the same employer for the duration of your co-op, unless a special situation arises, like changing your major, which may mean that you are placed elsewhere.

Although you don't pay tuition during your co-op periods, you may need to pay a small fee, a requirement that varies from school to school.

In addition, if you co-op away from school and from home, housing can usually be arranged with the employer. Many of them offer subsidized housing or help with housing expenses. Alternatively, you may choose to take a position close to home to save in housing costs.

Example of a Work/School Co-Op Alternation Plans

School term	Plan A	Plan B	Plan C	Plan D	Plan E
1st year Fall	School	School	School	School	School
1st year Spring	School	School	School	School	School
1st year Summer	Work 1	•	•	•	•
2nd year Fall	School	Work 1	School	School	School
2nd year Spring	Work 2	School	Work 1	School	School
2nd year Summer	School	Work 2	School	Work 1	•
3rd year Fall	Work 3	School	Work 2	School	Work 1
3rd year Spring	School	Work 3	School	Work 2	School
3rd year Summer	•	•	Work 3	School	Work 2
4th year Fall	School	School	School	Work 3	School
4th year Spring	School	School	School	School	Work 3
5th year Fall	School	School	School	School	School
5th year Spring	School	School	School	School	School

• Optional Term (s) – Extra Co-op Work Term(s), Internship(s), Study Abroad, Summer Job, etc.

*"No matter how many hours you have to work,
you should remain an active student even if it means taking
only two classes a semester. It is vital to get a degree."*

—Jennifer L. Quijano

Internships

Internships are among the most valuable experiences you can explore while in college because they can provide you a glimpse of different careers and real-life jobs. Offered by many companies year round and during the summer, some internships are paid and others are not. The difference between an internship and a regular job is that you are more likely to learn about an industry or a career during an internship than at a regular job. Given the type of jobs you are probably going to land while you are in college, an entry level, basic position, an internship is a better alternative because your boss understands you are there to learn something that will impact your future. (In this respect, it's a similar proposition as a co-op job with the main difference being that you would usually intern full time during the summer or part time while you are in school.)

Although it's not the most common case scenario, some people are very lucky and they get a job early on in their area of interest. This is what happened to Teri Arvesu, the Executive Producer of Noticias 23, Univision in Miami, Florida. "During my spring break as a junior in high school a friend of the family who was doing some freelance work with Telemundo asked me to help so I could get some experience. I met the woman who became and, continues to be, my mentor. She opened many doors for me and continued calling me back for other freelance jobs while in high school and college. I did an early internship in the newsroom as freshman in college and continued freelancing thereafter. By junior year in college I had my first full-time job at the network and remained very close to the contacts I made at the local level. Whenever they needed any help I was always available despite having a full-time job with the network and studying full-time."

Key Advantages of an Internship

- You learn skills and acquire experience in your area of interest
- You can usually arrange your work schedule around your school schedule
- It's a great place to network and find mentors
- You can verify that the field you are interested in is really what you expect it to be
- It may lead to a job offer

Every summer Leylha Ahuile, the founder of Tinta Fresca, either had an internship or a job. She worked two or three jobs most summers so that she wouldn't have to work that much during the year. "I was either going into pre-law or political science so, during my second year I interned at a law firm. It was good because within days I realized I didn't want to be a lawyer. The other jobs I had also allowed me to see what I enjoyed doing. And it is through one of these jobs —reading Spanish literature to a blind graduate student—that I discovered my career. Up until then I hadn't read any of the Latin American authors like Gabriel García Márquez, Julio Cortázar, etc. And because the Spanish editions were not available in Braille, I had to read them aloud to this student. That's how I discovered my passion."

Many high school students who come from homes with professional parents are likely to have had summer internships because these parents are able to open doors through their connections. Other students may have found their own internships through their high schools' guidance counselors or through other means. If you had an internship during high school, you already know the value it added to your college application. Well, that value is even bigger when you have internships listed on your college resume. Employers like seeing you took the initiative to learn about a particular industry and they also appreciate not having to hire someone who doesn't know the first thing about the work environment. If you didn't have the experience when you were in high school, this is definitely the time to seek it!

Carla Rivera, my personal intern two years ago and now a junior at Pace University, started her internships in the summer of her freshman year. "I met with the people at the Career Center and told them my major was journalism and that I wanted to get an internship," she shares. After her summer internship with me, Carla got one with ABC where she is still working about eighteen hours a week. She studies full time and is actively involved in the Latino Organization in campus plus she has an active social life.

The power of INROADS

To help you land an internship, there is a very important organization you need to know about: INROADS (www.inroads.org). Their mission is: *To develop and place talented minority youth in business and industry and prepare them for corporate and community leadership*. This international organization, founded in 1970, has 50 offices serving more than 4,500 interns at over 400 companies. Their model is unique in several ways. Let's take a look at it.

1. The internship

INROADS offers paid corporate internships. They last between two and four consecutive summers (8-10 weeks) at the same company and the goal of the internship is to ultimately offer you a job.

There are several requirements for you to be selected for the program:

- You must set and achieve personal and academic goals

- You must plan to pursue a degree at an accredited four-year college or university (or you must be attending one already)

- Maintain a B (3.0 GPA) or better average and remain in good standing with your school

- You must attend all INROADS corporate training in June and July

- You must stay in touch every month with your INROADS advisor

- You must fulfill 8-10 weeks of internship to the satisfaction of your corporate sponsor and INROADS

- You must do community service every year

Wilson Martinez del Río, Industry Vice President, Energy, Manufacturing and Technology at INROADS says: "The community service piece is key. Companies want to hire self-directed people who can be leaders, not just good technical professionals. We found that community service allows students who are shy to come out, and those who are more outspoken to learn to listen. It really helps develop their talents and leadership skills."

2. A three-way partnership between the company, the INROADS advisor and the student

What's unique about INROADS' internships is that they offer you a wonderful platform to start your career early. The direct access to the corporate world, the networking opportunities, the training, support and guidance you receive are powerful tools you don't find so easily elsewhere.

The corporate sponsor provides a three-person team: A supervisor who is there throughout your internship and helps you develop goals, gives you an evaluation at the end, etc.; a mentor who stays in touch with you during the year and advises you on company culture and on your professional career; and a Human Resources professional who is the liaison between INROADS and the sponsor company.

An INROADS advisor will be assigned to you according to your major. He/she will help you with work-readiness issues year-round, he/she will discuss with you what clubs you should join in school, what courses you should take and how to best take advantage of your internship. This unique team helps you develop as a person and a professional throughout the internship and is constantly supporting your objectives and monitoring your progress.

"If you are struggling in college, high school or any other level, use all the support that your school offers (student clubs, counseling and academic assistance, tutoring, etc.)! That's what they are for and it's probably included in your tuition anyway! Make your family proud of your efforts, but more importantly . . . make yourself proud of achieving what very few are able to."

—Miguel R. Olivas-Luján, Ph.D., Professor of
Business at Clarion University of Pennsylvania

The Power of the Hispanic Association of Colleges and Universities (HACU)

In your quest for internships, HACU (www.hacu.net) is another important organization with which you should become familiar. HACU helps Hispanic students obtain paid internships in corporations and government offices.

Their internship program is open to undergraduates and graduates enrolled in any four-year institution whether their college is a HACU member or not.

The eligibility requirements are:

• Minimum 3.0 GPA (on a 4.0 scale)

• Be enrolled in an undergraduate or graduate degree program. (A senior graduating in May is only eligible for the summer program.)

• Completion of the freshman year of college before the internship begins

• Authorized or eligible to work by law in the United States

HACU's largest internship program is during the summer. "The internships year round are for students who take a semester off school to work full time," explains Ana Esquivel, the Executive Director of HACU Corporate Internship Program and Student Services. "They can get academic credit for their internship but they have to work it out with their academic advisor," says Ms. Esquivel.

According to previous HACU surveys, around 85 percent of students get a job offer before the end of their internship so they go back to the company after they graduate. "Nowadays, having internships within the field of study is very important because it exposes students to the basics of the industry, the terminology, etc. In addition, some universities are now requiring the completion of an internship before graduation," says Ana Esquivel.

You can find details on HACU's internship program plus students' testimonials on their website. See the Chapter Resources for more information. And don't forget to review the internship resources offered by SEO (Sponsors of Educational Opportunity) that I shared earlier in the book when I talked about Careers of the Future.

Finding a Job That Fits Your Goals

There are job opportunities out there that can lead to a career in a company. The key is to identify your interests and to work as professionally as possible regardless of what job you get. Even when you work as a crew at a fast food restaurant you must strive to be the best worker: Be punctual, work hard, help your co-workers, have a positive, can-do attitude and be grateful for the opportunity.

You can make a difference at any level of the organization and you can get noticed for your good work. Getting noticed for exceptional work leads to promotions.

When Jobs Work Out Well

Margaret Lazo, the Senior Vice President of Human Resources at NBC/Universal Cable and Entertainment, who was a communications major at St. John's University in Jamaica, New York, did an unpaid internship at CNN as a junior while working at Macy's through college. "I did my internship for course credit and worked at Macy's because my parents paid for my tuition but I paid for everything else. I worked as a part-time sales associate and progressed to being an evening and weekend supervisor during my shifts at the department store until one day the Human Resources manager there asked to see me. He asked me if I'd like to pursue a career at Macy's noting that I communicated well and that I had demonstrated I managed my co-workers well, and he suggested a career in Human Resources by explaining in detail what he did in the Human Resources department. He became my first mentor. After going through an interview process with their corporate offices, I was offered a position in their executive training program. The program was a 10-week course designed to develop merchandising executives so I was the unique candidate and was then placed as a Human Resources Manager in their store in Stamford, Connecticut when I completed the program... I was 21. Eight years later, I got a call from a recruiter representing NBC which was a uniquely perfect fit providing an opportunity to grow as an Human Resources professional in an industry where I had originally envisioned my career path going.

Whether you need a year-round job or a summer job, you need to follow these same steps.

Steps to Finding a Job that Fits Your Goals

1. Make a list of your areas of interest (if you haven't declared your major, and you are interested in several things, list them all).

2. Talk to your counselors and professors so they can help you identify jobs where you could develop skills and experience in your field(s) of interest.

3. Look for directories at the library or search the Internet to identify companies where you can interview for jobs.

4. Contact the personnel department at the companies you selected and find out if they have employment opportunities for college students.

5. Create a resumé with the help of your Career Services office and submit it along with a cover letter.

6. Schedule interviews.

7. Before you go on an interview, practice the questions they will ask you with your Career Services counselor.

8. Send "thank you" notes following your interviews.

Importance of Sending Thank You Notes

You have no idea the impact that a little handwritten "thank you" note has on a person! Employers interview people all the time, so those who send a note after the meeting stand out. Here's what you note should cover:

- Refer to the date when you met and to the position you discussed

- Thank the person for their time

- Tell them you are interested in working/interning for the company

Keep it short, polite and make sure it has no grammatical or spelling mistakes!

Example of How it Works

Say you are interested in communications, marketing and public relations. With the help of your advisor, you realized that you could benefit from working at a marketing or PR agency, at the marketing department of a large corporation, at the Press office of an elected official, or at the PR department of a large foundation. You then look for a business directory in your area or you contact the local Chamber of Commerce to provide you with a list of organizations that fall within your parameters and you begin to make your phone calls and schedule your appointments.

How to Find Jobs On Your Own

Start by using the Career Services office at your college; they usually have multiple partnerships with businesses in the area. Then talk to everyone you know and ask them if they know someone who may have a job opportunity for you in your areas of interest. Talk to professors, upper classmen, your classmates, family and friends. But also, drop by small companies in your area and ask to talk to the manager to inquiry directly. Don't underestimate the power of showing up in person. When you do, make sure you are dressed professionally and that you bring your resumé with your contact information clearly printed.

Chapter Resources

www.aftercollege.com—Provides internships and entry-level job listings for current students and recent college graduates.

www.avenidaUSA.com—Is the first directory of Hispanic college graduates in the U.S.

www.collegegrad.com—Offers access to entry-level careers for college students and recent graduates.

www.nyu.edu/careerdevelopment/alumni/alu_additional_resources/alu_job sites.php—The Career Development section of New York University's website offers a wonderful list of job search sites. Many of them are general job search boards but there are many others specialized by industry.

www.getthatgig.com—Offers links to employers and other websites where you can find industry specific jobs.

www.INROADS.org—The INROADS website will clarify any questions you have on how they match students to internships.

www.hnip.net—The Hispanic Association of Colleges and Universities National Internship Program's website. You will find all the information about HACU's internships.

www.hispanicheritage.org—The Hispanic Heritage Foundation (HHF) identifies, inspires, promotes and prepares Latino role models through national leadership, cultural, educational and workforce programs. They offer scholarships and a program called LOFT (Latinos on Fast Track) that can help direct you to great paid internships and job opportunities.

www.seo-usa.org—Sponsors of Educational Opportunity offers several programs. Their Scholars Program recruits motivated students of color in NYC public high schools to help them realize their full potential. All of the Scholars in the Class of 2007 are attending a four-year college. Scholars are awarded scholarships and thrive in competitive colleges. This program provides services and support in grades 9 through 16. Their Careers program is a summer internship program for talented students of color leading to full-time job offers.

www.toigofoundation.org—The Robert Toigo Foundation's mission is to encourage more minority presence at senior levels across all areas of finance. They recruit the best, brightest and most committed minority students pursuing finance-related careers. Toigo Fellows (first or second year MBA students) receive tuition assistance, mentors, coaches, career counseling, leadership training and a host of formal and informal networking opportunities.

Books

How to get a job in the U.S., A Guide for Latinos by Mariela Dabbah (Sourcebooks, 2005).

Resumés for Dummies, by Joyce Lain Kennedy (Wiley, 2007).

Resumé Magic: Trade Secrets of a Professional Resumé Writer, by Susan Britton Whitcomb (Jist, 2006).

Best Resumés for College Students and New Grads: Jump Start Your Career by Louise M.Kursmark (Jist, 2005).

Get a Job! Interview Survival Skills for College Students, by John R. Cunningham (Paperback, 2005).

Getting to 3rd Base: A College Student's Primer to Getting the Interview, Getting the ob, by Jim Fiorelli (Paperback, 2003).

The College Student's Step-by-Step Guide to Landing a Job by Mike Krush (The Samuels Intellectual Capital Group, LLC, 2005).

The Complete Job Search Book for College Students: A Step-by-Step Guide to

Finding the Right Job by Richard Walsh and Michelle Soltwedel (F + W Publications Inc., 2007).

Vault/INROADS Guide to Minority Entry-Level and Internship Programs, 2007 Edition by Vault Editors (Paperback, 2006).

For more information and a constantly updated list of resources log on to **www.latinosincollege.com**.

Chapter 10

SOCIAL LIFE ON CAMPUS

Meeting all kinds of people and participating in all sorts of activities is a big part of your college years. This rich experience will vary according to where you go to college and it will feel differently depending on what your high school was like.

For instance, if you attended a large urban high school you were probably exposed to students with very diverse cultural and ethnic backgrounds whereas you may have not had a lot of exposure to students from a diverse economic background or from different countries. If you went to a small suburban high school where most of your peers where white and wealthy, you may not have been in contact with students from other ethnicities or who come from lower income families.

The same is true for college. Depending on the type of school you attend you will be one of a handful of minority students or one amongst a large population. For instance, if you are at a large city college most likely you will see a substantially diverse student community. And if you attend an Ivy League school, you will probably see lots of foreign students as well as lots of students from wealthy families.

WORDS OF ENCOURAGEMENT

"Youth are often referred to as the leaders of the future, but why wait until the future? You can be a leader today by getting involved. Step out of your comfort zone and get involved in activities that benefit your peers."

—Gregorio Hallman Jr., the doctoral student

What's important is that no matter where you are, you try to meet as many people as you can. This is the time to develop relationships that will last a lifetime and many people who didn't use their time in college to do so, have badly regretted it. Diana Baez, Coordinator at American Express Company and Custom-Fashion Designer, who graduated with an Associate's Degree in Fine Arts and Fashion Design from the Fashion Institute of Technology in New York, comments: "I didn't want to be distracted with friends and peer pressure, but I actually regret it now. It's so important to have good contacts and friends to share your sorrows with and grow with. If I had to do it again, I would join a group on campus."

So, get ready to enjoy your years in school and to meet people because there is a lot more to college than hard work!

Tips on Meeting People

If you are an outgoing person, you will have no problem meeting people in class and outside of class in clubs and organizations. But what do you do if you are on the shy side? Here are a few tips to help you break the ice.

✓ Seek out places where you can meet smaller groups of people such as certain clubs, study groups, or associations.

✓ Focus on meeting just one person at every place you go.

✓ Invite your new friend to go with you to the next event. While at that event, introduce your friend to the other people you meet and ask your friend to introduce you.

✓ Ask your new friend to invite you to some of the activities he/she is involved with.

The secret is to go places with someone you know, and, once you arrive, to avoid hiding in a corner with this person. By introducing each other to other individuals you take away the need to introduce yourself, which can be difficult for some people.

Gladys Bernett, a business consultant and owner of Intercontinental Trade, LLC, who has a Master's degree in Health Care Administration and an MBA from the University of Florida, a school with over 50,000 students, says that it was hard to make friends in such a large campus. "The best way to meet people with similar interests in a large school is by becoming involved in activities, so I got involved with the board of college council and with other professional organizations. This allowed me to not only meet people who were focused professionally but allowed me the opportunity to develop leadership skills while building my resumé. Also, students have a tendency to be friends, roommates and take classes only with people who come from the same country or have the same cultural background. For example, there was a group of Koreans in my school that hung out only with other Koreans or Panamanians who hung out with other countrymen. I don't recommend this. I think you have to be open minded and meet people from other cultures. I'm from Panama and I had friends who were Pakistani, Thai, Greek, African American, etc. This allows your college experience to be a lot richer and after you graduate you will be able to do business and have friends everywhere in the world."

You can actually apply Ms. Bernett's suggestion to any size school. Participating in activities, sports, student organizations, and so on, is a wonderful way to meet people who share your interests. Besides, students who get involved in extracurricular activities above and beyond what's required, tend to be more interesting people, and they also tend to become leaders in their own fields. As your relationships develop and deepen with the years, you will realize that having a vast network of friends, who, upon graduation move to different parts of the country, will be a great asset for your career. These are the people who will occupy key positions in key companies and organizations and who will help you advance your career goals just as you will help them advance theirs.

The truth is that one of the best assets you have when you graduate from an Ivy League school and from many of the top schools is the network. Individuals who attend Harvard University, for instance, are part of a network of alumni that rely on each other for everything from getting job recommendations to finding apartments in the most sought after locations, amongst many other things. They organize dinners and fundraising events where they continue to network with each other and they have access to an email database that is like a directory of some of the most powerful people in America. When they meet people in a social or professional event and they find out they are Harvard alumni, they establish an immediate connection and willingness to help one another.

This effect is also true of most alumni who attended the same university. Once you discover someone attended your Alma Matter, you are both more likely to be open to lending each other a hand, a reaction similar to what you would have if you both belonged to the same professional association or supported the same charitable cause. But the strength of the networks at the top schools is undeniable and that is why I encourage you to attend the very best school for which you qualify and that at the same time, matches your interests and personality. Once again, what you obtain from such an experience far outweighs de financial sacrifices you might have to make at first.

WORDS OF ENCOURAGEMENT

Michael G. McKenzie Jr, the Information Technology Analyst at Morgan Stanley, who is now obtaining his Masters of Science in Information Systems at Pace University, says:

*"Stay focused and believe in yourself.
Don't ever be afraid to ask for help because you will
be surprised at how many people are willing to help
you if you are willing to put an effort."*

Where to Meet People

In every college there are a large number of groups you can join, where you can meet all sorts of people. Some of them are:

- Fraternities and sororities
- Social activism clubs
- Intramural sports, recreational teams
- Cultural clubs
- Political clubs
- School newspaper
- Arts clubs
- Professional associations on campus
- Leadership development groups
- Academic clubs
- Student associations

Within each one of the categories listed here, there are usually dozens of groups at each university. For instance, the University of California at Berkeley lists 83 groups under "Cultural" (including groups such as: Hermanos Unidos, Latin American Student Assocation, Mujeres Activas en Letras y Cambio Social, Students of Color in Public Policy and others) and 73 groups under "Professional" (including groups such as: American Institute of Architecture Students, Bioengineering Honors Society, Latino Pre-Law Society, Entrepreneurship Club, and others). So as you see, you can find your pick.

David Peña, Jr., the Executive Director of the National Hispanic Business Association and a graduate of St. Edward's University in Austin,

Texas, shares how he dealt with this issue in his particular situation: "My university didn't have any fraternities. However, through my scholarship and the network set up for the migrant students, I was able to create a network of great friends and supportive professors who understood the challenges of being a first generation college student from a migrant background."

And Miguel R. Olivas-Luján, Ph.D., Professor of Management at Clarion University of Pennsylvania, talks about the kind of activities he got involved in that enabled him to meet like-minded people: "Along with my friends we competed for and won the leadership of the student organization for our major. Part of the responsibilities included organizing a major student symposium as well as a software contest and that gave us the opportunity of doing unstructured projects and leaving our own mark on the school."

Meeting People Who Are Different

We all have a tendency to hang out with people who are from the same cultural, ethnic, religious or social background as us. The truth, however, is that the more you step out of your comfort zone to meet people who are different from you, the better prepared you will be to join the workforce in the future. So, besides hanging out with your Latino friends, try to join groups whose members don't look like you or don't think like you do, so you can learn from them. They will enrich your life and expand the way in which you see the world and they will help you realize that although you may have different customs, habits, beliefs, thoughts, political positions, and so on, you still have more similarities than differences. And that is a very important lesson to learn early on.

Marisela Riveros, senior TV producer, who graduated from Montclair State University in New Jersey, comments that she didn't join a sorority in her school because she didn't identify with the ones in her campus. But she found two wonderful ways to meet people doing something she absolutely loved. "I joined the Latin American Student Organization (LASO) and the school's radio station WMSC 90.3 FM. I had so much fun! I would do it all over again if I were asked. The LASO office was full of music and life! I joined the publicity department and at one point they wanted me to be the head of publicity. I didn't take the job because I became more involved at the radio station, something that had to do a lot with my career. I became the first Hispanic to host a Spanish-language show at the school's radio station. We were seen as the wild kids since I came with my Latin House, salsa and merengue music to host: 'Latinos in the House' every Wednesday from 12-2 PM between class breaks. My friends at LASO listened to my show and all of a sudden four guys approached me to be trained. They too wanted to be radio DJs. So, I became the station's multicultural director."

WORDS OF ENCOURAGEMENT

Miguel R. Olivas-Luján, the professor of management at Clarion University comments: "*I used to feel that fancy jobs with international travel were only for those born to the right families, but before I was 25 I had one. College gave me the opportunities that showed me that I can do anything I want to do; it was really a matter of deciding what I wanted! I eventually found it in my career as university professor where I do research that improves companies, I teach students that soon become tomorrow's professionals, and I travel around the world sharing my work with colleagues from other nations."*

Meeting People When You Don't Live on Campus

As you read in previous chapters, attending a community college while you work, or commuting to school from home may impact the social aspect of your college experience. But now that you know it, you can do something about it!

Remember that these are very important years to develop your social network. So, don't look at school as a place where you are only getting your academic education but rather as a place where you are also getting your social connections. Make time to join clubs and organizations where you can make friends. If you don't have much time to spare, choose one or two activities that interest you and stick to those. A study group for example, could be a wonderful place to help you achieve both your academic and social goals.

If you are one of the many people who are working to pay for college and you feel like you want to get your school over with as soon as possible, think again. Most people who went through college like that regret not having taken the time to build their social network. This is an incredible opportunity to meet people of your generation that will continue to grow and develop alongside you for years to come. Think about it this way: You are surrounded by future heads of companies, business people, politicians, professors, scientists, and artists who will manage and change the world. Wouldn't you want to meet as many of them as possible? Well, this is your chance!

To Greek or Not to Greek

An interesting peculiarity of the American university system is the existence of social organizations called fraternities (often called "frats") and sororities. Fraternities are usually all male or mixed-sex organizations while sororities are the female-only equivalent. Because the names of these organizations generally consist of two or three Greek letters, they are collectively known as Greek Societies and their members as Greeks. There are some exceptions to the use of Greek letters and those include some secret societies at some of the Ivy League schools.

Many Latino students find that Greek life is not for them. I wonder if they are aware of how many different fraternities and sororities there are in each campus and how much Greek life varies from school to school. There are Greek houses known for heavy partying every night, while others have clear rules separating study time and party time. There are alcohol-free co-ed houses and there are even many Greek organizations that focus on Latinos and African Americans.

Undoubtedly, the main reason why people join these organizations is to have a sense of belonging and to expand their social life. Lulu Wang, the graduate student who is currently getting her MBA at Harvard University, shares her regret for not having joined a sorority when she was at Boston University: "Even though I participated in some of the pledge events I didn't feel connected to sorority sisters. However, not belonging to a sorority isolated me from the students who tend to sign up for fraternities/sororities, and who are predominantly Americans. Later on during my career at Deloitte, I found out that brothers or sisters of the same group tend to use their networks to help each other; they form strong bonds because of the similar experiences that they go through in college. When I first started my job, my peers were referencing the same insider stories, jokes or anecdotes that I could not relate to. It was hard to break into the group."

Carla Rivera, my former intern, decided to bring a Latino sorority to her Pace University Campus because she felt there was a lot of partying going on in the other sororities. "I believe there's more meaning in cultural sororities than in social sororities. Becoming a member is more difficult because you have to learn your history, your culture and then, to be initiated you have to perform certain tasks." And even though bringing a new sorority to campus is an uphill battle, to her, belonging to a sorority has a lot of benefits: "People develop much stronger relationships when they belong to the same sorority or fraternity," she says.

This is a feeling shared by some people who were members of Greek organizations. Jose R. de la Torre, Professor at Florida International University and a graduate from Penn State, who grew up in Cuba, says: "I did pledge and join a fraternity and it was a great experience for me. It provided me with a network of people that would have been difficult to develop on my own. Living in the fraternity house for nearly three years surrounded exclusively by Americans, allowed me to integrate into U.S. society in a way that would have been very different (or at least much slower) otherwise."

Speaking Greek

✓ "Rush" is the term used for the period in which people visit various Greek houses to meet members. This period, which usually happens during the first semester of the school year, is sometimes called "rush week."

✓ "Rushees" are the first year students who participate in the "rush". (Many students decide to participate in the rush just to meet fellow freshmen and upperclassmen and then decide not to accept the bid.)

✓ "Bids" are the invitations sent to students by Greek organizations inviting them to join.

✓ "Accepting the bid" means the student wishes to join a Greek organization. Once a student accepts the bid, he/she becomes "a pledge" of the organization.

✓ "Pledge period" is the period during which "pledges" find out more about the fraternity or sorority and make a final decision o join. You have to be prepared to interview with the other members, go on scavenger hunts and other time-consuming rituals. You also need to pay a fee that varies according to how much the national organization requires and how much the local chapter charges for dues. You may be asked to do public service, wear a pledge pin, and learn about the history of the organization. This is the period that used to be associated with hazing which is defined as a ritualistic abuse, harassment or persecution of individuals in a group. It once involved activities such as branding, using drugs, kidnapping, sexual favors, etc., that have been banned from most campuses.

✓ "Initiation" is the formal ceremony through which someone joins the sorority or fraternity and it often includes secret ceremonies and rituals.

✓ "Sister and Brother" are the way in which members of the same sorority or fraternity refer to each other.

Let's talk a bit more about pledging. This is the period when a student who has pledged to the Greek organization is put to the test. It's still associated with all sorts of unpleasant activities such as doing calisthenics in your underwear in the middle of winter, drinking enormous quantities of alcohol at once, and worse. And although hazing has been barred from most campuses, it still goes on and every year there is at least one death related to hazing in fraternities/sororities.

Some organizations have suspended rogue chapters for breaking the law but sometimes that has made the situation worse as the chapter doesn't have to go by the rules of the organization any longer. That's why your research before you join is crucial.

According to Dr. de la Torre, fraternities and sororities might have more value if you are attending a school in a remote area because they may offer the only means of socializing whereas if your school is in Chicago or in Los Angeles, you have all sorts of other alternatives to meet people. "I was in Penn State, in the middle of nowhere and I felt pretty lonesome. In the fraternity house every Friday or every other Friday we would have a "social" where we invited a sorority so we could meet girls," Dr. de la Torre explains.

It's important to keep in mind that being part of a fraternity doesn't mean that you can't also join other groups. Many people think that once you join a fraternity or a sorority you limit your access to other individuals, but that is exclusively up to you. Dr. de la Torre, for example, was a member of the choir and of the Engineering Society where he met other friends with other interests; he also met friends in his different classes, just as you will.

With the number of alcohol-related incidents in many fraternities and sororities still taking place across the country, maybe the best thing to do would be to spend your freshman year evaluating the Greek organizations at your school and whether it is worth it for you to join. Find out which ones are alcohol-free, which ones have gotten into trouble, which ones are involved with community projects, etc., so that you can make an informed decision and not just join one because your friends do. Without a doubt, the main reason to join one of these organizations is to expand your social network. Make sure it doesn't come with a high price tag attached. And if, at any point, you are involved with a Greek organization where there's any kind of hazing going on, do report it to the school administration. This is the only way that we can stop these sometimes horrific practices from continuing to happen.

To help you decide what will feel more comfortable for you and what makes the most sense, check some of the pros and cons of pledging to a Greek organization.

Pros and Cons of Pledging to a Sorority/Fraternity

Pros

- ✓ You build strong relationships that last a lifetime
- ✓ You get insight into the American culture that might take a long time to acquire otherwise
- ✓ It's a good way to develop a strong network, sort of your extensive family
- ✓ They afford you a sense of belonging
- ✓ There are upper classmen members to whom you can turn for help or advice

Cons

- ✓ In some fraternities/sororities there may be excessive partying and alcohol consumption

- ✓ There are still some incidents of hazing being reported in campuses across the country. Some of them end in death, others, in serious injury. For example: Alpha Tau Omega on the University of Nevada, Reno campus, was accused and proven guilty of hazing during the spring semester of 2008 because some pledges were branded on the buttocks and sought medical treatment.

- ✓ Regarding living in a frat house: It may be tough to live in closed quarters with 30 or 40 people

- ✓ There is a cost involved in joining and some extras like gift giving, etc.

- ✓ They seem to work better for party/social type of students

- ✓ They are generally considered superficial and divisive

Meeting people during your years in college is as important a priority as doing well in your classes. Make sure you get involved in the right places and activities so you hook up with positive, interesting, bright students and avoid at all costs getting into trouble. Learn about the realities of Greek life before you either join an organization or discard it.

CHAPTER RESOURCES

www.nalfo.org—The National Association of Latino Fraternal Organizations is an umbrella council of 23 Latino Greek Letter Organizations. Their goal is to promote positive inter fraternal relations, communications and development of all Latino fraternal organizations through mutual respect. See the list of organizations in Appendix 1.

www.stophazing.org—Provides information about hazing in college and other places.

www.nicindy.org—North American Interfraternity Conference provides information about going Greek and support for their member organizations.

www.facebook.com—Facebook is one of the most popular social networking websites for college students.

www.migente.com—Mi Gente is a social networking website geared to Latinos.

Books

The Real Freshman Handbook: A Totally Honest Guide to Life on Campus by Jennifer Hanson (Houghton Mifflin, 2002).

Confessions of a College Freshman: A Survival Guide for Dorm Life, Biology Lab, the Cafeteria, and Other First-Year Adventures by Zach Arrington (River Oak, 2008).

Inside Greek U: Fraternities, Sororities and The Pursuit of Pleasure, Power and Prestige, by Alan D.DeSantis (The University Press of Kentucky, 2007).

Wrongs of Passage: Fraternities, Sororities, Hazing and Binge Drinking by Hank Nuwer (Indiana University Press, 1999).

For more information and a constantly updated list of resources log on to **www.latinosincollege.com**.

Chapter 11

ROOMMATES

If you grew up in a typical Latino household, you were probably surrounded by your direct family plus your cousins, aunts, uncles, grandparents and close friends of the family. People stayed over at your place and your parents hosted large meals and celebrations on a regular basis. You are probably used to sharing your living space with others and may have even shared your bedroom with one or more of your siblings. Well, this training will come very handy if you decide to live with a roommate.

Although in the beginning your new roommate may be a stranger and you may need to set up some rules for living together, being open with each other and respectful are two important traits that will help you get along.

If you are still in high school and you are considering going away to college, thinking about how to prepare for your life with a roommate is an important part of the process. If you are in college, you may already have some experience with this topic and you may just need some help dealing with this reality. Read on and you'll find the section that best suits your current needs.

There's More Than One Way to Slice a Cake

First let's look at the different ways in which you can choose or get a roommate.

1. If you live on campus, your school will assign you a roommate. You may have some say in the matter but not much.

2. Most recently, some schools have set up a website where you can search for a good roommate match after you fill out a form.

3. If you want to live in an apartment off campus, (usually only allowed after your freshman year) you may use websites like **www.Roommates.com** where you post your add looking for a roommate to share your apartment or you search for someone who already has an apartment and is looking for a roommate.

After you are assigned a roommate, you may look him/her up on social networking sites such as Facebook or MySpace to learn more about the person with whom you'll be sharing at least a year of your life. Be careful to jump to conclusions based merely on this person's Facebook's page. First, because it's important to get to know your roommate in person before you decide he/she is the wrong match for you and second, because most colleges won't allow any changes until after you lived together for a while. So bottom line, you have to give this person a fair chance, because you'll most likely be living together, whether you are happy about it or not.

In some colleges, students are creating groups based on residence halls and floors where they share information and tips about their new home. Finding out about these groups and joining them may be a great way to get to know your classmates before you move in.

Things to Consider If You Rent an Apartment with Roommates

1. If you are thinking of renting an apartment first, and then looking for someone to share it with you, I suggest that you pay special attention to the following points:

   • Check the lease to verify that you are allowed to have roommates and whether they need to be approved by management. Many places require that you add the name of your roommate to the lease and others require a full credit and background check.

   • Find out how the deposit works. What happens if your roommate causes damages or breaks the lease? How will this affect you?

   • Ask your roommate for a deposit. If he/she breaks the lease and leaves, you will still be held responsible for paying the total rent at the end of the month, and you want to cover yourself in case this happens.

   • How does having a roommate affect your renter's insurance?

   • Are pets allowed? What about smoking?

   • Are visitors allowed?

2. If the lease is under someone else's name you need to check:

- Will you have your own assigned parking space? (If you have a car, this is important because some apartments allow for only one spot for the person on the lease.)
- If the apartment complex has a gym, will you have full use of it? What about other amenities?

The Voice of Experience

Jocelyn Acosta, a premed junior student at Cornell University in Ithaca, New York, who transferred last year from SUNY University at Buffalo shares: "My experience in Buffalo was absolutely amazing! I loved every part of it. I was an Acker Scholar, which is a scholarship for minorities from disadvantaged communities or low economic status. I lived in a suite with eight girls, all of us Ackers and all of us were either black or Latina. We got along very well. I never experienced racism. Personally, I think it's essential to be within your own race to establish a sense of ethnic identity."

Items to Discuss Before You Move In Together

Moving in with people you barely know requires that you establish some clear rules ahead of time. The clearer the two of you are with each other, the better. I'm sure it is close to impossible to find someone with whose habits you agree 100 percent, but talking about your likes and dislikes early on will definitely help. So, whether you are moving into an apartment with roommates or to a dorm on campus, here are a few things you may want to clarify.

- Will you only split the rent or will you also split the utilities, food and other household expenses?

- What level of cleanliness are you used to? Can you agree on how neat you will keep the place?

- How will you keep the apartment clean? How often will each of you clean common areas and your own rooms?

- What time does each of you go to bed? Do you need peace and quiet when you go to sleep or can you sleep through an earthquake?

- Do you or your roommate work at night and sleep during the hours when the other person is active in the apartment? Talk about your schedules: People with very different schedules may not be a good match.

- Some ethnic foods can have a strong smell. If one of you enjoys that kind of food, how tolerant will the other one be? Do you have to restrict the cooking to a certain number of days a week? What will the policy be in terms of leaving food around the house?

- Regarding food, will you do the grocery shopping together or separately? Will you have different areas in the refrigerator? Will each one of you only be allowed to eat what you buy unless the other one offers to share?

- What will be the policy about visitors? Will they be allowed overnight? If family comes to visit, how long will they be allowed to stay? If one of you has visitors all the time and the other one doesn't, it can easily create resentment.

- What will the noise policy be? Will you use headphones to listen to your music and watch TV late at night or when the other person is studying? Will you have a "silence after certain time" policy?

- Do any of you have pets? Is the other person okay with that? Any allergies?

- Are you and the other person from two different cultures? Do any of you observe specific rituals? Are you and is the other person okay with this?

- What are your bathroom habits? When do you shower? Do you keep a clean bathroom? How often will each of you clean it?

- What are your study habits? Do you study at home, and if so, do you do so in your room or in a common area? Do you study in the library?

After you discuss all these different points, I suggest that you write a living contract and you both sign it. By writing it together you are ensuring that you will both try to follow it. When one of you breaks a rule, and this WILL happen, make sure you apologize and move on. There is nothing worse than harboring resentment towards the person you share a home with.

If instead of an apartment, you share a dorm, you can still review most of the topics listed above so you can come to certain agreements. Granted, there's less wiggle room when the school assigns you a roommate than when you choose who will share your apartment, but there are many things that can make the experience a more positive one.

Setting ground rules together and writing a living contract will be a big step towards achieving a harmonious coexistence.

More Tips On Choosing the Right Roommate

When it comes to roommates, being compatible is more important than being friends. Moreover, do you even know if you'd be able to room with your best friend? Making sure that your lifestyles don't collide is more relevant than sharing the same taste in clothes or movies.

So, although there's something to be said about liking the person with whom you are going to share at least a year of your life, you don't need to be best friends in order to have a comfortable living arrangement.

During your first conversation on the phone, listen for clues that may reveal things about your roommate that escape the list I shared above, but keep you focus on how compatible you are. Ask your questions and set up meetings with the people you really like on the phone.

WORDS OF ENCOURAGEMENT

Arturo Poiré, Senior Vice President, Head of Talent Acquisition at Marsh Inc., says: *"I think Latinos have everything to be successful in the American system, and there are plenty of statistics to prove it. I'd like them to show, in the way in which they approach education, more of that focus and work ethics that made their parents and grandparents sacrifice so much to be a part of America. I want Latinos to be known for how well they do in school and how rapidly they are going up the ranks in every profession. It can be done."*

Living with Someone From a Different Culture

I'd like to look at this particular aspect in a little more detail because chances are that you will be rooming with someone from a different culture. Clearly, this means you will most likely have some things in common as well as a number of differences. As I pointed out above, before you decide to live together, it's critical for both of you to learn something about each other's values, habits, rituals, etc.

For instance, if members of your family plan to visit you often, do they expect to stay with you? Is this okay with your roommate? Or, if you like to play your music loudly, does this bother him/her? And how will you deal with someone from a very uptight upbringing who doesn't talk about her feelings, keeps to herself and doesn't like to share much of anything? What about with someone who only showers once a week? Or someone who prays several times a day? Talking about these issues and projecting your life together for a year in small quarters, may help you figure out if you are a good match for each other.

The Voice of Experience

Carla Rivera, my former intern, had the same roommate during her sophomore and junior years.

"She's an African American girl and we are very different people. There are a lot of cultural things that are hard to adjust to. So, the key is to keep open communications, which we do."

Lulu Wang, the student currently attending Harvard University to obtain her MBA, comments:

"I think if you are an international student or someone from another culture it would be beneficial to have an American roommate. The relationship can help both of you to broaden your horizons."

When Things Go Wrong

Even when you like your roommate and you set all the rules ahead of time, it is quite possible that things will go wrong from time to time. (I'm sure you've heard your share of horror stories.) It is advisable to have a regular roommates' meeting, maybe once a month, to discuss issues that are problematic. Having these regular meetings gives you a formal space to talk about bills, chores, disagreements, etc., and to resolve any disputes before they escalate, or before the electrical company shuts off your electricity for lack of payment!

Here's one of the many bad stories I heard. It's about Carla Rivera's brother, who attends Loyola University in Chicago. "My brother rooms with two kids, one of which parties a lot. One night, when my brother was sleeping, one of his roommates had friends over for a party where they did a lot of drinking and drugs. One of the guests spilled water on my brother's laptop and ruined it. They gave my brother some money for it but my brother complained to his RA. The RA asked my brother to write a report for every time his roommate did something bad and he in turn gave it to the RD (Residence Diretor), who is an adult in charge of the building and who reports directly to Residential Life. They had to write several reports against this kid before they moved him out of my brother's room."

If you ever get into a similar situation with your roommate, always involve your RA as early as possible to seek advice and to find out the proper steps to follow. This way, you are not prolonging a situation that may become unbearable and might affect your morale and your ability to concentrate on your studies.

Finding Solutions to Frequent Problems

Here are some ideas on how to approach a few of the most common problems with roommates.

Problem	Solution
One roommate does most of the chores around the apartment	Create a master chore list with the name of the person responsible for each chore. Determine for how long you will do these chores and after that period is over, switch responsibilities.
One roommate is messy and the other is neat	Agree that common areas of the house will be kept neat and individual rooms can be kept as the owner wishes.
One person keeps piles of unwashed, smelly, laundry all over the place	Decide on the day of the week you'll do laundry together to motivate the other person to go with you.
One person uses his/her roommate's things without permission	Establish clear privacy boundaries and a rule that if something breaks while it was in the wrong hands, that person will pay for the damages. This should also apply to your guests.
Disputes over food/drinks left all over the apartment	Make it a rule that food belongs in the kitchen area to avoid mice, and other undesirable vermin.
One person has people sleep over all the time	Set up/review rules of who can stay over: relatives, boyfriend/girlfriend, people you date, etc.

If you share a dorm, adjust the above solutions accordingly. For instance, there should be no food left outside of your refrigerator; you should establish clear "neatness" rules as basically your entire space is common space, etc.

Steps to Resolve Disagreements

Okay, so you have a list of problems and a list of ways in which you can deal with them. Does this mean the solutions I'm giving you will work all the time? No! It just means there are ways to solve each problem and the ones I'm offering may trigger some ideas that may work even better for you. But the truth is that things don't always work out the first time you try them and you may need to tweak your approach to get some results. So, here's how to handle a difficult situation and how to step up your efforts if the problem persist.

Step 1

It's very likely that as part of your Latino heritage you have a strong inclination to please everyone and to avoid conflict whenever possible. So, here you are, in a conflicting situation trying to be nice. My suggestion is that you use your strong diplomatic skills to politely speak to your roommate about the problem right when it starts. Don't wait until you can't take it anymore because by then, your resentment and anger will do most of the talking. Try to express how the situation makes you feel while you avoid accusing the other person. For example, say something such as: "When you leave food and garbage in the living room it makes me feel like we live in a dump. Would you mind putting the leftover food in the refrigerator?"

Step 2

Okay, so you spoke up and the food is still all over the place except, obviously, where it belongs. What now? Write a note. A short, polite note that you should write after the anger passes (usually, after a good night's sleep!). "Laura, I really appreciate your efforts to keep the leftover food in the refrigerator. In the last few days, however, I'm noticing food in the living room again. Would you mind continue putting it in the fridge? It really helps! Thanks, Cristina."

Step 3

Discuss your problem during your monthly meeting. Make it part of your official agenda and point out how serious the situation is for you. Again, focus on how it makes you feel and avoid calling your roommate names.

Step 4

Enroll the help of your RA. They are used and trained to help you deal with all sorts of situations like this, so they can help you develop a strategy. Moreover, they will discuss with you the procedure to change roommates, if that is what it takes.

Living on the Study Hall

Choosing to live on the same floor with people who are studying the same major as you has many advantages. Leylha Ahuile, the founder of Tinta Fresca, who lived in the political sciences floor, shares some of the advantages here:

- You have students from freshmen to seniors living together, which gives you access to people who can help you with your questions at any time of day or night because they're older than you.

- There's a greater sense of community and camaraderie.

• Professors take you more seriously because you are living on the floor with other people interested in the same subject as you. They know you're committed to your studies.

So, if your college offers this alternative, it may be worth looking into it.

Regardless of what your living arrangements are, whether you live on or off campus, every time you have roommates you have to be prepared to make some adjustments. Keep an open mind and be positive about the situation, as living with roommates will prepare you to deal with many other situations in life. Embrace it as a learning experience!

WORDS OF ENCOURAGEMENT

Cristina Pinzon, a freelance reporter/producer,
who recently graduated from Montclair State University
in Montclair, New Jersey, says: *"I would tell Latinos,
and everyone for that matter, to believe in success. I truly believe
that motivation is key in finding one's career path, but you
will find many times that your belief will be tested by negativity.
I would recommend young individuals to surround
themselves with people who share their ardor. Surrounding
yourself with people who take great pleasure in their
work will help you nourish your own passion."*

Chapter Resources

www.roommates.com—A great site to find roommates.

www.collegeview.com/articles—A wonderful resource for articles on all topics including what to bring to college and how to make the most out of a small space.

www.facebook.com—One of the most popular social networks for college students.

www.myspace.com—Another very popular social network where you can search for your roommate's page.

Books

Rules for Roommates: The Ultimate Guide to Reclaiming Your Space and Your Sanity by Mary Lou Podlasiak (Writers Club Press, 2000).

The Naked Roommate: And 107 Other Issues You Might Run into in College, 2nd edition, by Harlan Cohen (Sourcebooks, 2005).

My Roommate Is Driving Me Crazy! Solve Conflicts, Set Boundaries and Survive The College Roommate From Hell by Susan Fee (F + W Publications Company, 2005).

For more information and a constantly updated list of resources log on to **www.latinosincollege.com**.

Chapter 12

TIME TO LEARN HOW TO MANAGE YOUR TIME!

Maybe you think this is the first time that you are on your own in terms of managing your time. But if you look back, you'll see that you did lots of that during your high school years. Juggling school, your extra curricular activities, your social and family life was a great practice run for college. And if you worked part time or had some internships to boot, you may already be a master of time management.

College, however, presents its own challenges because you have some fixed times, your classes, and a lot of free time in between—if you don't work. There's no question that in order to succeed in school, you must learn how to manage your time. The trick is to find the right balance between studying hard, socializing, working or participating in an internship, volunteering in organizations, getting involved in extracurricular activities, exercising and so on.

For many Latino students who have to work during college, balancing their lives can be more than difficult. Luz Canino-Baker, the managing director of programs and marketing at HACE, got her MBA at the University of Chicago and her Bachelor of Science degree at DePaul University, also in Chicago, while she worked full time. "For years while I was in school I lived by quarters (ten weeks) and that carried with me for years after I graduated. In other words, I set goals in ten-week increments. As for working full time and going to school part time it took tremendous discipline. There was no time to hang out with friends, no time to read magazines and books I wanted to read."

And, if on the one hand, having a work schedule and a school schedule have forced these people to be extremely organized, on the other hand, achieving a balance was quite stressful.

Marisela Riveros, the senior TV producer says: "My parents could only send me a limited amount of money a month (they lived in Venezuela while she was in school in New Jersey), so I had to work at the school's cafeteria. My mom doesn't know it but I didn't have a balanced diet at all. I ate a lot of ham and cheese sandwiches and many days my breakfast was a Green Valley Granola Bar and an orange juice box. All of that was very stressful."

But working while going to school is not the only challenge you will have to overcome in order to have a balanced life. The temptation to party and hang out with your friends all the time may also be a factor, given that you are around them all the time. So, it's important to surround yourself with driven, hard working individuals who share your goals and commitment and who push you to excel.

Latino Time

I'm sure you are familiar with the reputation Latinos have for not being very punctual. Here's Arturo Poire's take on it: "As I always say, if you are Latino and you are late, you are 'more late' than anyone else and people assume that you are late because you are on 'Latino time' (which in my case is not true). There are many stereotypes that is important to be aware of and manage." This means that in order to avoid feeding into the stereotype, you need to be more punctual than anyone else!

Tips to Get a Handle on Time Management

Although the task of managing your activities in school can seem daunting, there are a few things you can do to be more in control. Let's take a look!

1. Attend a Time Management Session at Your College

Most colleges offer this class and you would be wise to take it early on. If you haven't taken it yet, maybe it's time to do so.

2. Prioritize

How do you figure out what's less important when everything right now seems to be on the top of your list? I know that you want to experiment all sorts of new things and it's hard to choose, but it's critical that you do. Be selective in the number of activities you commit to so that you are not overscheduled as this will lead to stress and underperformance. If you work and study at the same time, try to be realistic about how much more you can take on. Yes, it would be fantastic if you could join a student association or be the editor of the school paper, but only commit to doing it if you still have time left to study, exercise and relax a little bit. Having some time off is just as important as everything else.

Learning to Say No

One of the most typical Latino traits is the difficulty to say "no". We like to please everyone and at times that behavior leads to a disregard for our own needs. If you are a good student and have great leadership skills, you will be asked to participate in all sorts of events and to assume all kinds of positions within different organizations in school. It will be flattering and it will be hard to refuse the honor, but if you accept all that is offered to you, eventually you won't be able to deliver on your promises. So, choosing which activities to get involved with and which ones to decline is the key not just to keeping your schedule balanced but also to keeping your commitments. Learn to say "no" graciously and save yourself lots of stress and broken promises.

"Managing time is the part of growing up that is the hardest," says María Clara Naranjo, Program Director, Southeast Outreach at the Hispanic Scholarship Fund, who graduated with a B.S. in Family and Consumer Services from the University of Georgia, Athens, GA. "Yet, now I'm a professional and it's an essential part of a successful career, therefore an important skill to learn in college."

Make a Daily To-Do List

To help you prioritize, try using a daily to-do list. Just thinking about the top things you need to write down on the list will help you clear your mind. You may want to keep a weekly "to do" list where you include academic deadlines and other things that need to be taken care of, and then move some of those items to your daily to-do list.

Mark those tasks on your list that are urgent with an "A" and the less urgent ones with "B" and "C". This way you can always focus on finishing your "A" tasks first. Cross out the items as you complete them.

The bottom line is: Prioritizing is about knowing yourself. What is important to you? What are your goals? What are your passions? These are things only you know and you need to think about them as you sit down with your to-do list and with your calendar.

Creating a daily list could become your morning ritual. You should sit with a paper calendar that lists the hours of the day and determine how many hours you have committed to class and how many free hours you have left. Then you can itemize the things that you need to do, from studying for an exam to buying food and doing laundry. Next, put a priority letter next to the item. Next, decide exactly when you will take care of the items on the list.

WORDS OF ENCOURAGEMENT

María Clara Naranjo, the program director, Southeast Outreach, of the Hispanic Scholarship Fund, shares: *"College is one of the most rewarding experiences in anybody's life. Everybody needs to go through a transition from child*

to adult and college is a great structure for that.
If you are in school and you are struggling to finish, keep the
faith and remember the motivation that got you there.
Everybody needs to find an outlet. For me, my religion kept
me grounded, especially at my most trying moments."

3. Use a Calendar

I know it sounds obvious, but do you have a calendar? Writing things down will help you keep your life organized. There are several free online calendars you can use if you rather not use a paper calendar. Put your test dates, paper due dates and other deadlines in your calendar and then calculate backwards how many days you will need to study or do research for that particular deadline. Assign enough hours ahead of time so you don't have to pull all-nighters. (Most experts recommend that you set aside two hours of study for each hour of class.) Look at the Chapter Resources for information on free tools available online.

4. Avoid Procrastination

If you often find yourself putting off the things that you should be doing right now, you're probably a procrastinator. And although we all go through this stage from time to time, if it is a pattern of yours, you should look into it and try your hardest to modify it as it will not just affect your studies but your professional career.

Many people procrastinate because they don't have a clear idea of how much time the task will take. They leave it for the last minute thinking they have enough time to complete it, only to realize they don't have enough time. Others wait for the right mood to strike them before they sit down to work. Whatever your reasons for leaving things for the last moment, I suggest that you try to shift your thinking. Plan ahead and leave time to review your work and relax as the deadline approaches. You will notice a relief in your stress level and a new sense of control over your life.

To break the procrastination cycle, which is usually more noticeable the farther away the deadline is, "attack" any large project right away. Even if you do something small, starting with the project will get you over the thought that: "This can wait". So, as soon as you get the project, do some initial research, write the opening paragraph of a paper, schedule an interview with someone you want to consult on the topic, etc. I personally, find it easier to come back to a project I have already started than to come back to face the "white page" of a big project. For instance, if I have a conversation with a client and I decide that I need to develop a new Power Point presentation for their audience, I pick the template and title and I write the headers on all the slides right away. So, when I come back to the presentation a few days later, I feel like I'm continuing with the work I've started instead of feeling overwhelmed by all the decisions I need to make regarding the content, the formatting, etc.

5. Study Groups

Many people find that being part of a study group helps them manage their study time better. Miguel R. Olivas-Luján, Professor of Management at Clarion University in Pennsylvania, says: "For a while, I sacrificed my private life for all the projects I worked on, but most of the time, I actually enjoyed it! I used daily planners; I worked Saturdays and Sundays and I studied in groups to force myself to get things done."

Being part of a group can offer you valuable benefits. There is a commitment to meet on a specific day that forces you to be there. In addition, the opportunity to teach what you know to others in your group reinforces your knowledge.

Lulu Wang, the Consultant at Deloitte Consulting who is attending Harvard University to get her MBA, comments: "I prioritized my activities every week. If I knew an exam was coming then it was more study time than social time. I also worked with my classmates and friends. It was usually helpful to be in a small group working on a problem-set together. It not only helps academically but it also helps you grow as a person."

Be aware, though, that study groups only work when everyone is committed to studying and doing hard work. If you find that the people in your group waste their time gossiping, go back to studying on your own. It's possible that for you, the best way thing to do is to study on your own as much as possible and consult with others on issues that you don't understand.

6. Combine Activities

If it's time to do laundry, bring your books to study. If you know you are going to stand in line for a long time—whether it is to pay for your books at the bookstore, to register for a class, or to get concert tickets—bring your notes to review them. By combining activities you may be able to use some otherwise "dead time" to study, and in turn, to free-up some of your study time for relaxation.

Time Management Tips for Studying

- Clean up your space: Having an orderly study space will help you concentrate. And, while you are at it, make sure you have good lighting.

- Have everything you need before you sit down to study. Getting up to fetch books, notes, or other information is a waste of time.

- Study at the library: Yes, this old temple of knowledge can work wonders for your concentration and it offers less distractions than your room or your home.

- Keep it quiet: The brain can only focus on one stimulus at a time, therefore, if you are trying to read while keeping up with the baseball game on TV you are wasting your time. Your brain waves move from the page to the game and back. You think you are doing two things at a time but your brain is working at half speed so you are actually taking double the time.

- Study hard subjects first. We've all tried it, leaving the worst for last. But in reality, this strategy seldom works. You want to attack the difficult topics when you are fresh and not when you are tired. You'll notice you get the information faster, which will in turn save you some time.

- Study in shorter time blocks (30 to 40 minutes each) and take short breaks in between. Instead of sitting down for hours on end, this technique will help you avoid wasting time as a result of getting tired.

Use these strategies to improve your time management skills and you will soon see a big change in your stress level. And remember that the more you practice these techniques, the better you will get at managing your schedule, so be patient with yourself.

WORDS OF ENCOURAGEMENT

Diana Baez, the Coordinator at
American Express Company and Custom-Fashion
Designer, says: *"You can do anything you set your mind to.
I studied fashion and now I work for the Public Relations
department at American Express participating in
advertising and marketing meetings and providing my
creative input. Not in a million years would I have thought
that I could do what I love in a company
like American Express."*

CHAPTER RESOURCES

www.adprima.com/studyout.htm—Adprima, a wonderful site with all sorts of recommendations that will help you manage your time better.

www.google.calendar.com—A free online calendar to help you get organized.

www.myfreecalendarmaker.com—On this website you can print a free calendar in a variety of formats: daily, weekly, monthly and yearly.

www.keepandshare.com—This website offers free online and printable calendars as well as the option to share your calendar and to do lists with others.

www.mindtools.com—A wonderful website to get tips on time management, and tool such as a to-do list template and an Action Priority Matrix.

Books

Three Steps To Time Management For The College Student, CD, by Beverly Coggins (CD ROM, 2006).

Peak Performance: Success in College and Beyond. Tools For Time Management by Sharon Ferrett (Paperback, 2006).

How to Win at College: Surprising Secrets for Success from the Country's Top Students, by Cal Newport (Broadway Books, 2005).

For more information and a constantly updated list of resources log on to **www.latinosincollege.com.**

Chapter 13

CRASH COURSE ON MONEY MANAGEMENT

As soon as you hit your freshman year in college, you will be bombarded with credit card offers. Why? Because studies show that college graduates are faithful to the companies that issued their first credit card and that students represent a smaller risk than the general population. So, every other credit card company wants to make you their customer and most of them offer credit cards especially catered to college students. And although this is a wonderful opportunity to build your credit history, you have to be very careful with how you handle your cards if you don't want to dig yourself into a hole.

Given your age, you may have little experience managing money, and credit cards in particular. In addition, if you were raised with the idea that you should always pay cash for your purchases, your first goal should be to learn how credit works and how it could help you under the right circumstances.

Your Credit History

If you received or are trying to get student loans for college, you've already heard people talking about your credit history or your credit record. Most likely, you have none. Your record starts when you open accounts to your name. These could be utility bills, a bank account, a store credit card or a regular credit card.

If you pay your bills on time you will build a solid record. The same goes for your parents. The moment you start skipping payments, or paying late, your credit score goes down and your penalties go up! (And if your parents co-signed on a loan with you, their credit will also go down if you don't make the monthly payments on time!)

It's critical that you understand how important your credit record is because it will follow you for years. A good record will allow you to get loans, credit cards and eventually buy a car and a home. But if you have a bad record, which can take years to fix, many doors will be closed to you. And if this isn't incentive enough, bear in mind that more and more employers who conduct a credit check before they make a job offer. So your credit history can affect you more that you might have initially thought. It's not just about managing money, it's about establishing yourself as a trustworthy individual in the eyes of the many institutions you will have to interact with throughout your life.

Stretching Your Money

Paloma I. Veloz, the senior at Syracuse University, Syracuse, New York, who is studying journalism and international relations, shares a couple of tips for stretching her dollars: "I do my grocery shopping away from campus in the local supermarkets. It's generally cheaper because there are more sales, since that's were most people in the area shop. I'd also cook real food in my apartment. Generally, I'd make myself breakfast and dinner, because of my class schedule. This is not only a lot healthier, but you can get away from cafeteria food and have a nice, real meal for less money every week. Since I'm a coffee lover, I got myself a nice thermos and bought a coffee maker. Little things like that can get very useful in the long run."

How Credit Cards Work

A credit card is a financial instrument that is used in lieu of cash. It's a safer and practical way to pay for your purchases but because you don't see the actual money change hands, it can easily create the illusion that you can buy as much as you want because you can always put it on your card.

Your spending can get out of control very fast if you don't understand that whatever you pay for with your card needs to be paid back. All your expenses become part of your monthly balance on which an interest rate is applied. Which brings me to another illusion easy to succumb to: Thinking that paying the minimum amount listed on your card statement is enough. Not only it is not enough, but it can get you in serious trouble. **You should aim at paying the full amount every month.** (Yes, this statement is in bold letters for a reason!) Most cards have interest rates up to 25 percent on the unpaid portion of your bill each month.

Let's look at an example. Say you go shopping and spend $1,000 on your card, which has an interest rate of 15 percent. If you only pay the minimum payment, it could take you nine to ten years to cancel that debt! In addition, many cards charge an annual membership fee of anywhere from $20 o $100, they charge steep fees for cash advances (and sometimes a higher interest rate).

Andrea Sáenz, president of HACE, had a pretty bad experience with credit cards. "I accepted the offer my freshman year and managed it well until I went to Europe for the first semester of my senior year. After a couple of months, the money I had saved over the summer ran out because I was traveling, shopping and eating out a lot more than I would've if I had been at home. I started using my credit card for everything, including purchasing traveler's checks and exchanging them for cash. By the time I got back to finish my last semester in college I was in debt. I worked very few hours my last semester because I was writing a thesis and taking five classes, so I was making minimum payments on the card and using it to continue to eat out, shop and just live.

"When I graduated, I started out in a pretty low-paying job but I still had debt. Needless to say, my debt grew. It took a wake-up call from a financial advisor who I spoke with about three years after graduating to give me the discipline I needed to get out of debt. I consolidated all the debt on a zero or very low interest cards and moved it to a new zero interest-card whenever the introductory rate ran out. Every month I would say 'no' to invitations to movies or dinner with friends and instead put that money toward making large payments to the credit card company. I made the card payment a priority and within a year I was debt free. I've remained debt free (other than my mortgage and graduate school student loans) to this day, ten years later, by only buying things I can afford right now."

Reading the Fine Print

Many credit card companies set up booths at the beginning of the semester to attract students by offering T-shirts, teaser rates and other incentives to sign up. But before you do, check these items out:

- ✓ What happens after the teaser rate expires?
- ✓ What happens to your interest rate if you are late with a payment?
- ✓ What's the interest rate for cash advances?
- ✓ What's their annual fee?

The Right Way to Use a Credit Card

The best way for you to build a positive credit history is to get one credit card and to pay the balance in full every month. Little by little, the credit card company will increase your spending limit, which doesn't mean you need to constantly max it out! In addition, opening and closing credit cards frequently is not a good way to build your record. So, even when a store offers a discount on the merchandise or a gift for opening an account, don't do it if you are not a frequent client of that store.

The truth is, in order to control your spending, you will need to create a budget that takes into consideration your priorities and how much money you have available to spend after you pay for your food, books and other school expenses.

Also, keep in mind that some people receive their student loan money at the beginning of the semester and they misuse it. Then, they are left with having to pay with their credit cards for things that should've been taken care of with the loan. To avoid any credit problems, you may want to meet with a financial advisor and get some help devising a budget that works for you.

Other Ways to Build Your Credit Record

Credit cards are not the only way to build your credit record. There are other, sometimes safer, ways to accomplish this goal.

- Put the phone bill, gas and electricity and all other utility bills to your name. If you are sharing an apartment with a roommate, make sure they pay you on time because your record is the one impacted if you, for lack of funds, pay late.

- Open a checking and a savings account in the bank. The key here is to avoid bouncing checks! Usually, once you open an account the bank issues you a debit card. When making purchases with the debit card, the money gets deducted immediately from your account, so you need to make sure you are not left without funds to take care of bills that may come later in the month.

- If you don't qualify for a regular credit card, you can apply for a secured card. In this case, you deposit a certain amount of money with the card issuer and you charge against that cash.

Check your Credit and Your Wallet ... Often

If you loose your credit card or if it gets stolen, you should let the credit card company know as soon as possible. This will ensure that you are only responsible for a small fee (if any) and not for the expenses charged by someone else. (It's a good idea to keep a copy of your credit card on file so you can call with your card number.)

You also need to call the three main credit bureaus: Experian, Trans Union and Equifax (see their info in Chapter Resources), and let them know of the situation, in order to avoid the impact of the stolen card on your credit record. As a matter of fact, it is a good policy to request your free annual credit report from each one of these main three companies. In addition, if you suspect that you have been the victim of identity theft, you have the right to request these three companies to put a "fraud alert" in your file to avoid any impact on your credit report.

Visit the website for the Annual Credit Report to review the frequently asked questions **https://www.annualcreditreport.com/cra/index.jsp.**

Funny Stories You'll Remember

Samuel Ulloa, Director of Operations at Progress Financial, was always very good at keeping his credit cards under control. He paid his balance by the due date and kept track of his spending habits to better manage his money. "Like most college students, I also had very limited financial resources. I recall one time, that to stay within my budget I bought a sofa at the goodwill that was missing one leg. My roommates and I 'sacrificed' an unopened can of 'Rosaria refried beans', our humble food resource, to use it as the fourth leg on which to balance the sofa."

CHAPTER RESOURCES

www.annualcreditreport.com/cra/index.jsp—Annual Credit Report website, to request your annual free credit report from Experian, Equifax and Trans Union.

www.equifax.com—Equifax: 1-877-576-5734

www.experian.com/fraud—Experian: 1-888-397-3742

www.transunion.com—TransUnion: 1-800-680-7289

Books

Rich Dad Poor Dad for Teens: The Secrets About Money—That You Don't Learn in School, by Robert T.Kiyosaki and Sharon L.Lechter. (Warner Books and Little, Brown and Company, 2004).

The Motley Fool Investment Guide for Teens: 8 Steps to Having More Money Than Your Parents Ever Dreamed Of, by David Gardner, Tom Gardner and Selena Maranjian (Fireside, 2002).

Complete Idiot's Guide to Money for Teens by Susan Shelley (Pearson Education, 2001).

For more information and a constantly updated list of resources log on to **www.latinosincollege.com**.

Chapter 14

ACING SCHOOL

Of course this book would be worthless if you merely survive college rather than really ace it. So, it's time to get serious about how to succeed academically in the next few years.

Getting a college degree is very important but having a good GPA is also critical. Hiring managers at companies look at GPAs more than you think, so you really want to aim for a good average. The key here is not to obsess about your GPA or your grades, but to focus on doing exceptional work for every course that you take. If you focus on developing good study habits, in attending the lectures, and in putting your enthusiasm and passion in everything you do, you will be fine. And as I said earlier, if you have a job while in college, concentrate on keeping a good average throughout the courses of your major.

WORDS OF ENCOURAGEMENT

Due to a variety of circumstances, many Latino students arrive in college ill prepared for what is expected of them. Samuel Ulloa, Director of Operations at Progress Financial, shares his own experience: *"I was the first in my family to graduate from a four year university so I wasn't exposed to a typical college environment. When I first arrived in college, I felt alienated and a bit intimidated. Initially, I didn't know anyone who was of a similar background to mine—a migrant farm-working background. Even though I graduated Co-Valedictorian of my high school and I took all the advanced courses that were available, my classmates seemed so much better prepared than I was. They had the opportunity to take honors classes that were not offered at my high school. They had grown up with computers in their households. It quickly became evident that in order to do well I would need to close the 'knowledge gap' and that I would have to work harder and smarter than everyone else. Hard work, perseverance and resiliency became a driving force for much of my educational success. I began to develop these traits at the age of seven when my family and I immigrated to the U.S. in search of a better life, in search of the 'American Dream'. I feel blessed to have had the opportunity to get the learning that came along with the struggles associated with being a first generation immigrant, namely that one can accomplish anything that he/she sets their heart and mind on."*

Gladys Bernett, the business consultant and owner of Intercontinental Trade, LLC, suggests that you make an effort to get good grades right from the beginning because it will help open doors for you in the future. Focusing on getting good grades in your classes will also help you concentrate on your studies, something that may be hard for some students who get distracted by becoming involved in too many activities. "It doesn't matter if you don't know what you want to major in when you start college but stay focused in your school work. If you get good grades in your basic course work you will have more options of different careers to pursue. Maintaining a good GPA will be also very important to qualify for scholarships, internships and job applications upon graduation," says Ms. Bernett.

A good way to stay focused is by finding a good advisor to guide you; someone who can tell you which courses to take and which ones to avoid during your first semester in school to help you avoid unnecessary frustration. You will probably be assigned one at the beginning of your freshman year. Make sure you take advantage of this resource and develop a relationship that enables you to consult this person every step of the way on issues like your courses, your major, the clubs you should join, your research projects, etc. When you first start college, the temptation may be to explore everything on your own without anyone's help, but working with an advisor who can guide you will most definitely help you avoid some of the many roadblocks you may find along the way. Advisors are there to help, not to tell you what to do, so don't feel shy or intimidated.

Now, if you don't find an advisor in school with whom you are happy, reach out to professional organizations such as the Association of Latinos in Finance and Accounting (ALPFA), the National Society of Hispanic MBAs (NSHMBA), Society of Hispanic Professional Engineers

(SHEP) or find countless others in the Latin American Network Information Center (LANIC) (See websites under Chapter Resources.) These Hispanic organizations offer workshops targeted to college students and will help you find mentors and people who can guide you through college. I'm including a list of these organizations at the end of the book, so check it out.

Also, don't discard the mentors you had when you were in high school: The people who helped you get into college, fill out the applications for scholarships, edit your essays, or provided you with internships. There is no reason they cannot continue to be a part of your "support network" as you make your way through college, so be sure to stay in touch and offer them periodical updates on how you are doing, the challenges you are facing and the successes you are accomplishing.

The Voice of Experience

Let's hear Carla Rivera's tips on how to succeed academically:

✓ Always sit in the front row, in front of the professors. It helps you develop a relationship with them because they notice you more. If you need anything, they will try to help you. Personally, I've tried sitting in the back and you don't feel engaged in he discussion. Kids who sit there tend to fall asleep.

✓ Spend as much time with your professors as possible. Drop by the office, eat lunch with them and talk to them often. It really helps because you learn more about them and many of them become more like mentors to you, while others may even become your friends.

✓ If you don't do well studying by yourself, try a study group. For kids who are less motivated this works because they get encouraged to learn the material. I personally prefer to study alone and consult with my classmates when I need more information or before an exam.

✓ Trade-teach with others. Teaching one of your classmates who doesn't understand the material will help you learn it much better. Conversely, getting them to teach you something you don't understand will help them as well.

Just as you seek academic guidance from your adviser or mentors, you should seek it from your professors. By asking them for suggestions on how to do well and/or improve in their class you are opening yourself up for them to offer you their advice and you won't get any surprises when the final grade arrives. As Carla suggests, developing strong relationships with your professors is one of the best strategies you can implement to succeed in school. Although this may be harder to do in large, state universities, it is still doable if you persevere.

WORDS OF ENCOURAGEMENT

Alberto Ferreras, Creative Director/Partner of Latino Media Works, and the director of the HBO series Habla says: *"I would recommend any practical course that gives you exposure to the work atmosphere you will encounter in the real world. I think internships are invaluable. If you are a film student, go to the movies and analyze them with your friends. Take workshops, go to conferences and don't limit yourself to what is taught in the classroom."*

Study Habits

When it comes to study habits, it's hard to generalize because we are all different and things that work for some students, may not work for you and vice versa. There are, however, some strategies that seem to work for a large number of successful people and those are the ones I'm going to share with you here. If you feel time management is your issue, go back to Chapter 12 and take a look at my suggestions. Make sure you don't miss that information.

Student to Student

Here's a collection of study tips that students like you shared on various websites online regarding what works for them:

✓ Read over notes and then summarize them with your own words.

✓ Have a scent in the room when you study. Then wear that perfume when you take the test. It will help you remember because you relate the scent to the information.

✓ Listen to soothing but invigorating music. I usually listen to Beethoven.

✓ Keep peppermint in your mouth, it clears your nasal passages for more fresh air, which means more oxygen to the brain.

✓ Use flashcards.

Most people are shocked to discover the difference between studying for high school and studying for college. Even if you have taken AP or other honor classes, in high school teachers remind you of an upcoming test and they give you daily assignments. College, on the other hand, involves attending large classes with few daily assignments and a lot of "free" time in between classes. Your grades are primarily determined by midterms and finals and sometimes, the only place where you will find your due dates is in the course syllabus. This means that, if you haven't developed good study habits by now, you can't waste any time.

Good Study Habits

There are many things you can do to improve your academic performance. Paloma I. Veloz, the senior student at Syracuse University, suggests a couple of them: "I don't recommend all-nighters at all! As a college student it's easy to forget how important a good night sleep is to function well and to be productive during the day. I also try to study outside of my dorm, and instead study in a lounge or at the library. I find that I'm more productive staying away from distractions such as my T.V., my computer or better yet, my bed!"

Here's a list of ideas to help you improve your study habits:

- Set aside two hours to study for every hour of class. This will give you enough time to research and to read for the next test without leaving things until the last minute.

- Set up a daily study schedule that works for you. If after a short period of time you realize it doesn't work, adjust it.

- Start your study week on Sunday. Getting some work done before the actual work week starts, will help you avoid playing catch-up.

- Try eating protein foods to stay alert, for example: Lean meat, beans, lentils, low fat dairy, soy products, etc. Foods high in carbohydrates and fats will make you feel sleepy because they alter the amino acids entering the brain.

- Drink lots of water!

- Avoid drinking energy drinks to stay awake. Cristina Pinzon, the freelance reporter/producer and recent graduate from Montclair State University shares: "Caffeinated beverages can be detrimental to your coping with stress. From my past college experience I can openly say that drinking energy drinks kept me alert in classes but it also contributed to my anxiety attacks."

- Study in shorter time blocks (30 to 40 minutes each) and take short breaks in between. Instead of sitting down for hours on end, this technique will help you avoid wasting time as a result of getting fatigued.

- Use your breaks to walk, stretch and breathe deeply for at least five minutes. It'll get more oxygen flowing into your brain and improve your ability to concentrate.

- When choosing your course schedule, try to leave an hour between classes so you can review the material of the course right before you go in or right after you come out of class, when the material is still fresh.

- Nothing replaces studying, not even attending lectures. Some people actually find that they can't concentrate during lectures in huge auditoriums with hundreds of students. Instead of skipping the lecture, though, read the next bullet point for a better approach.

- Taking copious notes during lectures is a good way of staying alert (and awake!) during the presentation. Also, if you arrive early and sit up front, you are likely to get more out of it.

- To learn a wonderful system for note taking, review the Cornell Note-taking System developed by professor Walter Pauk and included in his book *How to Study in College, 9th Edition* (Houghton Mifflin, 2007). See Chapter Resources for the website. Through this system you will greatly improve your note taking skills something that, in turn, will help you with your study skills.

• Consolidate the notes you take during lectures with the material in the course text for a better understanding of the subject.

• Reading alone is not enough to learn the material. You need to understand what you read and sometimes the best way to do this is by taking notes as you read. This should help you make sense of the text.

• Highlight, rather than underline, important text. Studies have shown this technique to be much more effective for recalling information.

• After you have studied the assignment, talk about it aloud. Ask yourself questions about the text you just read and explain as much as you can aloud. It will help you see how much you understood and it will force you to go back to clarify any unclear points. You may do this with your study group as well.

• The above point can easily be mastered by developing a quiz and recall method to study with the goal of recalling all the information without checking your notes.

• Form your own study group. As long as you choose hard working students who don't spend most of the study time chatting or gossiping, it may help you stay motivated and focused.

• As I said in Chapter 12, use all your willpower to fight procrastination. Keep up with each course as you go so you don't fall behind and wind up scrambling at the end of the semester.

• Keep your materials organized by course so they are easy to find. Keep all the notes for one course in one binder.

• Study at a desk, never in bed! It will help you stay alert.

- Find a quiet place to study away from your room. Consider the Library as your first choice!

- For those times when you just can't get excited about a required course, try Samuel Ulloa's suggestion: "Speak to a classmate who is passionate about the material and find out why they are interested. Seeing things from a different perspective may spark your interest in the class."

- Do a little research before you choose your courses as professors make a big difference in terms of engaging your interest. (I'm sure you experienced this at some point in high school.) Alberto Ferreras, the Creative Director/Partner of Latino Media Works, advice on this topic is: "I would recommend students to be proactive in choosing their teachers. I prefer teachers who teach to think over teachers who expect you to memorize." Look for the teachers that will work best for you.

- If you choose a course that fails to excite you, drop it early so it doesn't get recorded in your transcript and you don't have to pay for it. Just make sure you drop it by the deadline.

WORDS OF ENCOURAGEMENT

"Success in school is like success in life: As long as you love what you are doing you will be successful."

—Leylha Ahuile, founder Tinta Fresca

CHAPTER RESOURCES

www.alpfa.org—Association of Latinos in Finance and Accounting.

www.shpe.org—Society of Hispanic Professional Engineers.

www.nshmba.org—National Society of Hispanic MBAs.

www.ipl.org/div/aplus/—Internet Public Library for Teens, offers help for high school and college students on researching and writing papers.

www.libraryspot.com/features/paperfeature.htm—Library Spot offers all sorts of websites with great advice for research and writing papers.

www.slu.edu/departments/english/research/—A Student's Guide to Research with the World Wide Web, teaches you how to do research on the net and how to evaluate the relevance, accuracy and authority of the material you find.

nutsandbolts.washcoll.edu/—Nuts and Bolts of College Writing teaches you from soup to nuts everything you need to know about writing a paper.

owl.english.purdue.edu/—The Purdue Online Writing Lab offers a variety of resources for all sorts of writing: research, academic, creative, etc. If your English is not perfect, you will find the English as a Second Language section useful to sharpen your language skills.

www.areasearchguide.com/—A research guide to help you with your term papers, your MLA style (Modern Language Association notation system), dealing with references, footnotes, endnotes, citations, etc.

www.mla.org—The Modern Language Association's site where you can learn more about MLA.

www.dianahacker.com—Diana Hacker's website. She is the author of several books about writing. If you have the book, the site offers links to companion student websites for each of her titles.

www.adprima.com/studyout.htm—Adprima, a wonderful site to read about study habits and to help you study for different situations: exams, recitation courses, etc.

www.clt.cornell.edu/campus/learn/LSC_Resources/cornellsystem.pdf—The Cornell Note-taking System, adapted from Walter Pauk's book.

lanic.utexas.edu—Latin American Network Information Center, offers a comprehensive list of Latino associations and resources from academic, to cultural, to community services, education, business, etc.

Books

How to Study in College 9th Edition, by Walter Pauk, (Houghton Mifflin, 2007).

How to Study, 6th edition, by Ron Fry (Thomson-Delmar Learning, 2005).

Study Smarter, Not Harder, by Kevin Paul (Self-Counsel Press, 2002).

How to Improve your Study Habits, by Waln K. Brown (Kindle Books, 2008).

How to Win at College: Surprising Secrets for Success from the Country's Top Students, by Cal Newport (Broadway Books, 2005).

For more information and a constantly updated list of resources log on to **www.latinosincollege.com**.

Chapter 15

TAKING ADVANTAGE OF WHAT YOUR COLLEGE HAS TO OFFER

I know it sounds obvious, maybe even ridiculous for me to spend one chapter telling you that you should take advantage of what your college offers. But you know what? I'm sure there are things you don't even know you could take advantage of!

Don't Overlook Opportunities

Loida Rosario, Marketing Faculty, Commerce College at DePaul University in Chicago, IL, says that Latino students tend to be shy about taking advantage of:

✓ Getting help from professors and peer students.

> ✓ Taking courses that would enhance their education such as writ-
> ten and verbal communications even if they are not required.
>
> ✓ Volunteering and building a network of people who once you
> graduate may be able to help you in your job search.

So to make sure that you don't miss out any wonderful opportunities or people who could be helpful to you at any given time, here's a list
of things for you to keep in mind.

Develop Leadership Skills
By Working in Various Organizations

As I'm sure you heard, employers everywhere look for candidates
with promising leadership skills. One of the best ways to develop this
trait is by volunteering in organizations and assuming leadership positions whenever you can.

If you live on campus, most Residential Halls have opportunities to
develop your leadership muscle at their Residential Hall Association, a
perfect way for you to get more involved with your hall while you pick
up valuable skills such as those needed for organizing events, presentations or discussion groups and those you need to help other students
with residential life.

But the truth is that in every college there are hundreds of opportunities to volunteer and you will find many of them in the organizations
I identified in Chapter 10. Academic, political or social clubs, student
organizations and professional associations all offer unique chances not

only to meet friends but also to develop skills that will prepare you for the workforce. Just make sure that you do more than participate in these organizations. You need to rise through the ranks to top leading positions in order to rip the biggest benefits.

For Samuel Ulloa, the Director of Operations at Progress Financial, as for many other people, some of the greatest learning from his college experience came from outside the classroom environment: "I joined several leadership roles such as captain of the intramural football team and president of the Society of Hispanic Professional Engineers. Taking on these roles taught me how to be an effective leader, influence others, time management, etc., all skills that have been instrumental in my career."

In addition, don't discount the possibility of creating an organization connected to any particular interest of yours and that still doesn't exist in your school. This level of initiative and creativity is what makes you stand out as a student and in the future, as an employee.

There are several organizations worth looking into when you consider volunteer opportunities outside of your campus. One of them is Junior Achievement Worldwide (www.ja.org), a great program that focuses on teaching students K-12 about workforce readiness, entrepreneurship and financial literacy through experiential, hands-on programs. You may have experienced their programs while you were in school! Well, it's a great place for you to volunteer your time while being a role model who inspires Latino students to pursue a college career themselves. They have offices throughout the country (and the world), they will train you to teach their programs, give you a kit with materials, offer lots of support and most importantly, they are very flexible with volunteers so, they will work with your schedule.

Seek Speaking Opportunities

Perhaps one of the best things you can do while you volunteer is to seek speaking opportunities. It doesn't matter if the occasion is to welcome freshmen into your organization, to present research findings or being part of a debate in class. What matters is all through college you develop your public speaking ability and you overcome any fears you might have. Try to take public speaking courses if they are available or to join a local Toastmaster's group. This is a crucial skill that will open lots of doors for you upon graduation and once you join the workforce. Did you know that public speaking is one of the top weaknesses that candidates bring up during a job interview? So if you work to gain command of public speaking, you will be that much ahead of everyone else.

WORDS OF ENCOURAGEMENT

If you are struggling with any aspect of school, here are some inspirational words from Loida Rosario, the Marketing Faculty, Commerce College at DePaul University in Chicago:
"You are not the only one. Seek help. Improve. Persevere. That's the meaning of success. But do not kid yourself . . . it's going to be hard and yet rewarding. The doors are opening more than ever in the U.S. for Latino students who excel in educational and professional performance, creativity and initiative. Seize the moment! It is yours for the taking!"

Develop your Writing Skills

I know you spend lots of time taking notes and writing papers. But I want you to also make sure you learn how to prepare a well-written article about a specific subject for publication. Take any necessary courses to help you sharpen the ability to communicate your thoughts in a clear and engaging way as this trait will come very handy when you join the workforce.

People who write well are in short supply and high demand. They are the people who can publish materials in professional publications and respected websites and become well known in a shorter period of time than people who can't write. In addition, if you can express your ideas well, it will be easier for you to influence others, a sure sign of leadership.

So, seek opportunities to publish Op-Ed pieces in the student paper. It will force you to first, choose a subject you know a lot about, and then polish your prose so that you stand out. Writing for the Op-Ed pages will have the additional benefit of making you better known in your school community. Other places where you can practice your writing skills while getting your name out there: Your student organization's, your local newspaper, the alumni magazine or your university's website, and any number of websites that could use content you're interested in writing about.

Study Abroad

Don't miss out on the chance to study in a far away land, to learn about a different culture and even a new language. Although coming from another culture, sometimes it may feel like you are *already* studying abroad, getting to thoroughly know (yet) another culture can be one of the most rewarding experiences in your college career. Many study abroad programs cost about the same as a semester in the U.S. and numerous schools will let you study abroad for up to a year. This is a fabulous way to travel and, given the increasing focus on employees who can navigate the new global economy, it makes your resumé look much more interesting. Give your international affairs office a call and plan ahead in order to fill out the applications on time.

Regarding this opportunity, Andrea Sáenz, president of Hispanic Alliance for Career Enhancement says: "I would recommend studying abroad to every student, even if it sounds like a big step. Just do it. Typically, college is the most flexible time in your life. You can pick up and leave town for a few months with relatively little disruption. Studying abroad gives you the opportunity to deeply experience life in a different part of the world, gain more independence and meet new people."

James Kopelman, the associate producer of After Ed.TV at Teacher's College, Columbia University in New York City, has an unusual story. Raised in Oklahoma in an English-speaking family, James, who is now fully bilingual, decided to study for a semester in Spain. "I wish more Latino students would take advantage of their bilingual background. It has opened doors for me in every job. I worked as a reporter, photographer and field producer for Telemundo from Oklahoma City. Who would have ever thought? When you are 18, 19 and 20 years old you don't know where you are going in life so you have to be exposed to as many experiences as possible because they will give you the biggest advantage. I NEVER thought studying abroad would help me. There's no way to know it until years later. But it did. I would've never been hired if I hadn't been bilingual."

Even if the cost of studying abroad is close to what you normally pay for tuition in your school, it may be hard to "sell" your parents on letting you travel so far from home. Gregorio Hallman Jr., who has an

American father and a Mexican mother and is currently studying for his Ed.D. at Teacher's College, Columbia University, New York City, found a great way to overcome this obstacle. "I asked my mother: 'How old were you when you came to the U.S.?' And she said: '19', which was my age at the time. And then I asked: "Why did you come here?" To which she answered: 'To have a better future'. So then I told her I wanted to go to Mexico to study academic Spanish so that I could have a better future too. It would open doors, and it would be good to learn about the culture and to develop a network. I essentially turned the tables on her and put her in my shoes. It worked."

Advantages of Studying Abroad

✓ Widens your view of the world

✓ Exposes you to different cultures

✓ You meet people from all over the world and forge strong relationships

✓ It builds self confidence

✓ You learn the language of the country

✓ You have unique experiences

If you decide to take on this incredible challenge, here are a couple of suggestions that might help you:

- Explore the one-year programs; they will help you develop better language skills and get more involved with the culture.

- Even though living with a host family is ideal for language learners, living on campus may offer a wider support net. Also, if you don't like your host family it may be harder to change it than changing dorms.

Network, Network, Network

I have said it many times and I will continue to say it: One of the most important things you need to do in school is to build a strong network.

Let me clarify what I mean when I say that you should "network". I don't mean to obnoxiously pursue guest speakers in search of a recommendation or a job offer. I don't mean approaching professors you admire to promote yourself hoping that they'll offer you a position in their department. What I mean when I tell you that you have to build your network during college is that you have to develop relationships. Honest, interesting connections with people around you to create a wonderful circle of diverse people with whom to interact now and in the future. They should be people who are in different fields of study, who have different personalities, but who you find inspiring, hard working, smart, open-minded, and who have high expectations of themselves and others. These are the people who will help you challenge yourself to be your best.

So, whenever you meet one of these individuals, never ask for anything. Be curious about their life and passions, offer help, time, or anything else you think they might be able to benefit from. Don't think of people in terms of how you will be able to use them now or in the future, but in terms of how much better your life will be with them in it.

I've already pointed out how fantastic an RA can be when it comes to finding support, information and advice on conflict-resolution. Don't overlook the other people in your hall if you live on campus, your classmates and friends, the professors, the guest speakers, the academic advisors, the coop services staff, and all the other administrators who actually work for you!

These are the people who are ruling and will continue to rule your world along with you for many years to come. The better you know them and the better they know you (this is the key!) the wider the range of opportunities that will come your way.

Imagine your life in five years, when you've been in your job for a while and are ready to move on. You send a few e-mails to your friends from school asking if they know of any opportunities in your field. Within hours a couple of them respond that they know of an opening in XYZ company. A few hours later another one of your contacts sends an e-mail saying she knows somebody who knows somebody who is looking for a person like you. You get in touch with the contacts and set up a few interviews. Before you know it, you have a new job without ever checking the classifieds.

This is exactly how things work in the real world. It's not always about submitting resumés and cover letters. First and foremost, it's about connections. Who you know and who knows you are key elements for your career advancement and that's why you want to meet as many people as possible while you are in school and create strong bonds with them that will last beyond graduation.

WORDS OF ENCOURAGEMENT

Margaret Lazo, Senior VP of Human Resources for NBC/Universal Cable and Entertainment says: *"You have to learn how to network. You need to connect with alumni and people from your guidance office and people you meet in internships. You have to do it through your years in college. Take advantage of every resource you have in front of you and network so you have people who are your sponsors all along the way and it's easier to get a job when you graduate."*

Regarding how important your connections with professors are, Henry Lescaille, Executive Director, of Human Resources, at Time Inc. says: "Someone once told me that professors are not 'personally' interested in their students (based on the size of some of the classes and the volume of students coming in and out of the school). So, early on, I didn't make a concerted effort to establish a one-on-one relationship with several professors. This was clearly not good advice—as professors do care about their students and the impact that they are making in their lives. Thanks to the relationships I ultimately made with several professors I was able to obtain a Presidential Scholarship and I was able to get 'practical experience' credits."

In addition, it's critical to know how to leverage other students on campus. "Many college students are not well socialized when they arrive on campus and they follow the same "clique" patterns they had in high school. Getting out of your comfort zone and meeting people who are older or more bookish or different in any other way expands your horizons and end up enriching the college experience," shares Rita Izaguirre, Human Resources Compliance Manager at GE Healthcare.

Consider also talking to your classmates' parents, as they may be wonderful sources of information right now and of recommendations in the future.

A Note on Social Networks Online

Using Facebook and other social networks online to meet people and stay in touch with your friends is perfectly fine. Just be careful with what you post as most employers are now checking people's pages on these sites before they extend a job offer. You want to avoid posting pictures, comments, blogs, and so on, that may be seen as unprofessional when it's time to get a job.

Approach Your Major Department

Once you pick your major, it's crucial to get involved with your Major Department. There are many ways in which you can do this: by attending the lectures they sponsor, attending thesis defenses, by going to their parties, and so on. It's important for the professors to get to know you. Getting involved will not only get you more psyched about your major but it will also convey the idea to those around you that you are serious about it. It will open opportunities to be a Teaching Assistant and to get good recommendations in the future.

Become Involved with Research

Many students don't realize that one of the main goals of their professors is to publish original research in the name of advancing knowledge. Being involved in this research from early on in your college career will help you not just get more enthusiastic about being in school, but additionally it will help you stand out amongst your peers.

You can get involved in research regardless of your major or field of study. Just approach the professors towards whom you feel more affinity and inquire about research opportunities.

CHAPTER RESOURCES

www.toastmasters.org—Toastmasters International is the leading organization in helping people become more competent and comfortable in front of an audience. They have clubs in every city so it's easy to join.

www.studyabroad.com—A wonderful resource on available programs to study, volunteer and intern abroad.

www.studentsabroad.com—A useful handbook for studying abroad which includes a checklist to prepare to study abroad, questions you should ask, country specific websites, and a lot more.

www.ja.org—Junior Achievement Worldwide is the world's largest organization dedicated to educating students about workforce readiness, entrepreneurship and financial literacy through experiential, hands-on programs.

www.iweev.com—IWeev is a "Multicultural Career and Netweeving™ Solutions Company". Netweeving™ is a next generation of social network application. It connects both professional and career-minded individuals in an environment of "each one teach one" for personal and professional growth. It gives its members the ability to form groups, build coaching and mentorship relationships and build knowledge and skills. It offers career services and online job boards.

Books

Make Things Happen: The Key to Networking for Teens by Lara Zielin (Lobster Press, 2003).

A Day in the Life of a College Student Leader: Case Studies for Undergraduate Leaders, by Sarah M. Marshall and Anne M. Hornak (Stylus Publishing, 2008).

For more information and a constantly updated list of resources log on to **www.latinosincollege.com**.

Chapter 16

YOU ARE YOUR OWN BFF!

Taking care of yourself while in college is crucial because if you burn yourself out, you will end up quitting. A lot of students focus exclusively on studying or studying and working and they forget that there needs to be time for socializing, exercising, sleeping and eating well if they are going to survive in the long run.

Stacey Martínez a full time student a Baruch College in New York City says: "Find a hobby that allows you to relax on your free time. Walking my two dogs helps me to relax after a long day. It clears my mind from all the stress of school and I just get to enjoy nature. Nature does wonders to soothe people." That is really good advice, so if you have a hobby, keep it up through your years in school. If you get a chance to practice a hobby outdoors, it would be even better. For instance, if you like playing chess, set up a game with a friend at a park. Or try to listen to your iPod while you take a walk by a body of water.

Stress

Many students feel stress. Whether it's related to your course load, to missing your family, to your job or to anything else, the truth is that it's quite likely that at some point you will feel stressed out and you will need to find a way to feel better. It's been proven that stress is at the heart of many diseases. Some people may develop headaches while others may get a skin rash and others may get diarrhea. And although these are real diseases that need to be treated, many times, the causes can be traced back to stress.

Identifying Symptoms of Stress

There are several ways in which you can manage your stress but the most important step towards success in this front is recognizing that you are suffering from stress! Here's a list of symptoms to watch for:

• Often feeling overwhelmed

• Feeling edgy

• Feeling irritated for no reason

• Having a short fuse

• Having low tolerance when things go slightly wrong or when simple things don't go as planned

• Being unable to focus or concentrate for long periods of time

• Being unable to sleep

• Feeling anxious all the time

• Overeating

• Loss of appetite

If you notice that you have some or all of these symptoms, you're likely experiencing some level of stress. Read on to identify the possible cause of the problem and check out some solutions to improve your situation.

Identifying the Cause of Stress

Although this is not a complete list of possible sources of your stress, it's a way to get you to think about what the cause might be. If you don't connect any of the causes listed here with what you are feeling, think about your very personal situation and what has changed during the last few months. Have you lost somebody you cared for? Have you taken on more responsibilities than last semester? Keep asking questions until you find the right answer and then, find a friend or a mentor who can help you brainstorm some solutions.

Here are a few symptoms that may be indicators of stress and some strategies you may want to try.

• **You're feeling time pressure**

Try to learn a few time management techniques from Chapter 11 and attend a class on this topic. Learning to manage your time is the key to diminish this stressor.

• **You miss your family**

Read Chapter 6 to get some ideas on how to deal with this issue and also talk to your RA to see if he/she has some suggestions on who to talk to in school.

• Your family is giving you a hard time

If your family is pressuring you in any way, whether it is to quit school and get a job, or to help them resolve other kinds of problems and this is becoming a distracting factor in your life, sit down and have a conversation. Muster all the patience of which you're capable of and explain how their attitude is affecting your academic performance and what the consequences of doing poorly in college will be. Try to establish clear rules by which they are not to call you to discuss certain issues or not to call you at certain times of the day. If this doesn't work, talk to your school advisor to get some guidance on how to deal with your family pressure.

• You have money problems

Develop a relationship with the financial aid counselor to seek as much financial help as possible. Get a mentor from one of the Hispanic organizations listed at the end of this book to help you manage your budget.

• You have job-related problems

Try talking to your supervisor to iron out any problems like scheduling conflicts, overtime demands that cut into your sleep and study time, etc. Also, consult with your coop services advisor as you may need to consider changing jobs or getting a loan to study full time. They may have good suggestions for you to implement.

• You feel anxious

If you feel short of breath, heart palpitations and dizziness, consult with psychiatric services. You may be suffering from anxiety and they will be able to help you. In addition, cut down on your caffeine consumption, including energy drinks and colas!

• You suffer from depression

If you notice symptoms such as being tired all the time, a lack of interest in activities you usually like and a change in eating habits, consult with psychiatric services. You may be experiencing depression and with the right treatment you can get well in a relatively short time. This isn't something unusual and you certainly don't have to face it alone. Look for help.

• **You feel like you don't belong in school**

Identify Hispanic organizations on campus and join. You can also get in touch with any of the Hispanic organizations listed at the end of this book to get help with this issue. You should also consider joining clubs and practicing activities that interest you such as sports, art, choir, etc. Getting involved with smaller groups will help you feel valued and it will enable you to make friends easier.

• **You have trouble concentrating**

Have a physical evaluation done by the clinic in your school and then, if it's appropriate, ask for a referral for counseling services. Try some of the ideas I shared with you in Chapter 14, as well.

• **You can't unwind**

Check your school's physical education programs and try to join a yoga class or any relaxation class. Try taking long walks in green areas and creating a special area in your house/apartment or room where you just relax. Set up a place with soothing music, a nice scent, some pillows and decide on a specific time of the day when you visit your special place. Once you are there, do nothing. Just sit or lie down and let your mind find a beautiful landscape (the beach or the mountains or whatever makes you feel relaxed). Breathe through your stomach using the technique I shared with you in Chapter 6.

• **You have persistent roommate problems**

If you are not able to resolve issues related to your roommate on your own by using the tips I gave you earlier, talk to your RA about maybe changing roommates or finding a more permanent solution. The sooner you deal with these problems, the sooner you can move on with your life.

• **Exam time is coming up and you don't feel prepared**

Sometimes this feeling comes from the procrastinating until it's actually too late to make up for lost time. If this is the case, review my suggestions on dealing with procrastination and consult your guidance counselor so he/she may help you develop a plan to overcome your tendency. If you never feel prepared enough and your grades are not as great as they could be, it may be part of a bigger problem. You may also want to consult your guidance counselor and hear his/her insights. Don't discard a consultation with a therapist on or off campus if the problem persists.

• **You're having trouble understanding the material and/or your grades are low**

Maybe your high school didn't prepare you as well as it could have for the demands of the college you're attending and you need to brush up on some of those concepts. Don't be embarrassed if you have to go back to some high school texts in order to comprehend your college materials. Even if you have to take some remedial courses before you can tackle the more sophisticated ones, it would be worth it. If you, however, feel that you should be able to understand the information and for some reason, are finding it difficult to do so, visit the student health center and talk to a mental health counselor.

Preparation, Preparation, Preparation

Cristina Pinzón, the reporter/producer, shares: "Preparation is essential in lowering the volume of stress you take on. I made good use of planners to remember upcoming events and thus prepare. Because my major required so much public speaking in forms of reporting, anchoring and acting, I discovered that preparing for these demonstrations made me less nervous and more comfortable."

Managing Stress

One of the best ways to manage stress or to keep it under control is by staying healthy. Yes, taking care of your body and your mind will help you manage your stress. When you walk, run, or exercise, you help your body lower the level of cortisol, a hormone secreted by your adrenal gland in response to stress. This hormone is involved in several functions such as regulating blood pressure, inflammatory response and immune function amongst others. And although stress isn't the only reason why cortisol is secreted, it's called "the stress hormone" because it's secreted in higher levels during the body's "fight of flight" response to stress.

Cortisol is a critical component of the body's response to stress, but allowing the body to activate its relaxation response is as important. When you experience constant stress (which may result in chronic stress), your body's stress response is activated so often that your body doesn't have an opportunity to return to normal. This means that you have higher and prolonged levels of cortisol in your bloodstream, something that has shown to have very negative health effects such as diminished cognitive performance, suppressed thyroid function, higher blood pressure, decreased muscle tissue, among many others.

Here are a few of the most effective ways in which you can manage your stress.

• **Eat well**

Eating well and drinking plenty of water helps maintain your organs in good shape and the oxygen flowing to your brain. So, the less chemicals you consume, the better your body will function. That means:

- Reducing the amount of carbonated beverages
- Reducing the amount of processed foods (they all contain additives, preservatives and other chemicals)
- Reducing the amount of caffeine (including energy drinks, chocolate and coffee)
- Reducing the amount of sugar and salt in your diet (that means, less candy bars, chips, etc.)
- Reducing trans fats (they clog your arteries)
- Eliminating cigarettes (they will kill you)
- Eliminating drugs (including prescription medication not prescribed to you!)
- Avoiding alcohol

Do I think that you will stop eating candy bars all together? No. But I'm suggesting that you try as hard as you can to eat as many unprocessed foods as possible in order to achieve better performance. Fruits, vegetables, eggs, fish, chicken, lean meat, and complex carbohydrates such as those found in whole grains, are all wonderful options to provide you with the energy you need to function at your best without imposing on your tight budget.

Also, making time to eat at a table, instead of wolfing down a sandwich while walking to class, can help reduce your stress level while it also helps you to eat less. As you focus on savoring your meal, you can better perceive when you are satisfied, something that's hard to do when you are walking or studying and eating distractedly.

• **Exercise**

Exercising is another key component of a balanced life. Very often, students forget that they have a body to attend to and not just a brain. For optimum brain function, exercise will increase the oxygen flow to your brain. So, make sure to fit in your schedule three or four times a week to do something physical. It can be a fast walk, a sport, or spending some time at the gym. Try to hook up with some friends for your physical activity as it will help keep you motivated and on a regular schedule.

• **Meditate**

If you don't meditate already, I encourage you to explore meditation. There are many places on the Internet where you can learn how to do it. See the Chapter Resources at the end for the websites.

Most meditation techniques involve finding a quiet place in the morning and in the evening where you sit crossed legged and focus your mind on your breath or on a mantra (a word or series of words you repeat over and over again). The idea is to train your mind to focus on just one thing while it lets everything else go. It's not easy to learn to think about nothing, to avoid getting attached to thoughts that rush into your mind the moment you sit to meditate. ("Oh, I need to finish my calculus assignment", or "I have to call mom and ask her to mail my library card.") But practice makes perfect and the more you meditate, the more control over your thoughts you get. And guess what? You will see a tremendous impact on your ability to study!

• Use Visualization Techniques

Visualizations are proven stress management techniques and along with "mental rehearsal" have helped people improve their performance in many disciplines. You may have heard of athletes who use these techniques to improve their time at a race, for example. They imagine shaving off seconds off their best 50 yards backstroke time, or going down the ski slope faster.

So, set a time every day when you practice being a successful student, acing the exam, getting into that internship you've applied for or anything else you wish to accomplish. Imagine every single detail of what you wish to achieve including your feelings at the precise instant when it happens; when you see the grade you received in your exam, for instance. The more senses you can engage and details you can visualize, the better. Soon you will notice that your stress levels are reduced and that your overall performance is greatly enhanced.

• Listen to Music

I know I don't have to tell you how much music can impact your mood. You know it. So, when you notice stress creeping into your life, take a break and retire to your favorite place to listen to those melodies that soothe you. Experts say that as you listen to music your heart beat will emulate that of the music, so if you are stressed, it might be a better idea to listen to soft soothing music rather than heavy metal!

• Get Enough Sleep

If you want to perform at your top level, you need to sleep well. All the studies show that when you are not well rested, you make more mistakes, and you have trouble remembering and learning. But although sleeping can help you deal with stress, many times stress itself is the cause of not being able to fall asleep. What should you do in this case? Learn a few techniques that will help you get your sleep such as: Avoiding caffeine and alcohol after 3 PM, drinking a glass of milk before bed, keeping your room dark during sleeping hours, etc. You can find more info on this at: **www.helpguide.org/life/sleep_tips.htm**

If none of these techniques bear results, I highly recommend that you go see your physician in order to get help figuring out what's wrong. Being tired all the time can be *extremely* detrimental to your studies so, don't let sleeplessness get in the way of your goals.

Partying

I'm not going to spend a lot of time here talking about drugs, alcohol and sex. I know you are aware of the effects and consequences of abusing any of these. Everyone around you has already told you, you see it everywhere, and you might even know someone who has gone down the wrong path. But I will say a few words to put in my two cents.

You may have already discovered (and if not, I'm sure you will find out soon) that some people can get really wild in college. They party 24/7 and spend little time studying, sleeping or doing anything else. These kids are very unlikely to succeed in college or afterwards, and associating yourself with this crowd, even when it may be the cool thing to do right now, will probably not benefit you in the long run. We tend to emulate the behavior of the people we are with, so why not choose to hang out with good students who have a clear idea of what they want to do with their lives?

Partying should be *a part* of your college experience and not the whole experience. So, as long as you keep a balance, you'll be fine.

As I said before, pulling an all-nighter is not recommended, so if you have a party coming up, you are better of planning to study ahead of time.

Underage drinking and drugs will quickly get you in trouble, no matter how "mild" you think they are. You can get suspended and expelled if you are caught, but more importantly, do you really want to invest money, time and effort and do poorly in school because you are under the influence? Think about it. You are dedicating a number of years to complete your college education. Wouldn't it be better to get as much out of school as possible? Staying healthy, sober and alert are keys to achieving success. That includes, not taking any stimulants to stay awake when cramming for a test. So that leaves you with two alternatives: Either you plan ahead so you don't have to cram or, you'll stay up all night on your own strength. I'd take the planning ahead any time!

And if we are talking about staying healthy, I can't avoid reminding you that smoking doesn't even look cool. If you don't smoke, congratulations! But if you do, quit today! Cigarettes are shortening your life one puff at a time. I know it's hard to quit as smoking is addictive, but there are all sorts of methods to help you achieve your goal, so talk to your doctor and find out which one would work best for you.

Sex

This is a delicate issue because many Latino families don't like to discuss it with their children (and because it has many religious implications that I'm not going to get into). As a result, you may have arrived in college ill prepared to deal with the reality around you.

Being away from home for the first time turns many teenagers into irresponsible individuals. They think that given that their parents are not around, everything's game so they may get involved in excessive partying, doing drugs and in irresponsible sex. The truth is, that you can ruin your life if you don't treat your recently acquired independence with respect. Your parents have trusted you enough to let you go away to school; don't disappoint them and don't get yourself into trouble.

Think carefully before you engage in sex and if you do, always practice safe sex. An unwanted pregnancy (regardless of whether you are male or female) can derail your education, and sexually transmitted diseases can mess up your health for the rest of your life. And although hooking up with different people in brief sexual encounters (whether they involve intercourse or not) sounds like a lot of fun now, it can become your worst nightmare if you are not careful. I'm including several resources at the end of the chapter for you to read. Please find someone on campus or off campus that you trust enough to talk about this issue.

Getting Sick

Everyone gets sick once in a while and you are probably no different. Many times, the stress, the lack of sleep, and the intense physical activity you are involved with are responsible for weakening your defenses and making you prone to catch any bug that's going around.

If you are away in college, it's important to realize that it's up to you to take care of yourself. Simple things, such as a cold, can be taken care of by drinking lots of liquids and getting plenty of rest. But persistent colds or headaches as well as any other disease require that you pay attention. Visit the school's doctor or, if you live at home, visit your own doctor to get help.

Being persistently sick will further weaken you and it will eventually impact your performance in school.

Trusting Yourself

I'm sure that you've gotten (and still get) your fair share of unsolicited advice from people around you. It seems like when people hear that you're going to college or that you are in college, they have an unbearable need to share their experience with you. Some even talk without having ever set a foot in college themselves! A lot of what they say will make sense and then again, a lot will not. Be open to what people that you respect and trust have to say and then test their advice against other people's experiences. In the end, when it comes to what will work for you, you need to learn to trust your instincts.

Here's a list of poor advice that students such as you have received:

• You don't need to develop a map of all your classes and schedule.

• Take "x" class and you'll get an easy A.

• Take courses in the afternoon so you can sleep late.

• Get over-the-counter stimulants so you can pull off all-nighters.

• Go to school as far away from home as possible.

• You are not smart enough for a four-year school; go to a community college.

• You don't need to attend lectures. Just borrow somebody else's notes.

• Hang out only with other Latinos on campus.

CHAPTER RESOURCES

www.helpguide.org—A non profit organization that provides information on health related issues.

www.webmd.com—A comprehensive health-related website where you can find answers to many of your questions.

www.healthline.com—A health care search engine.

www.how-to-meditate.org—A guide to Buddhist meditation made simple and easy to understand. It also offers a list of other Buddhist Websites and introductory videos.

www.learningmeditation.com—In this website you get the basics to begin meditating and some guided audio mediations you can play to start your practice right away.

www.collegesextalk.com—This website is a forum for serious conversation about sex in college. It's moderated by Dr. Sandy Caron and you can send her your questions.

Books

The Doctor's Complete College Girls' Health Guide: From Sex to Drugs to the Freshman 15 by Jennifer Wider, M.D. (Paperback, 2006).

The Dorm Room Diet: The 8 step Program for Creating a Healthy Lifestyle Plan that Really Works, by Daphne Oz (Paperback, 2006).

The Smart Student's Guide to Healthy Dorm Living: How to Survive Stress, Late Nights and the College Cafeteria, by M.J. Smith and Fred Smith (New Harbinger Publicaitons, 2006).

Hooking Up: Sex, Dating and Relationships on Campus, by Kathleen Bogle (New York University Press, 2008).

For more information and a constantly updated list of resources log on to **www.latinosincollege.com**.

Chapter 17

IS THIS SCHOOL FOR YOU?

There may be times during your college career when you will lack interest in what you are doing or lose sight of where you are going.

It happened to me. As I mentioned earlier, by design, college in Argentina is different than in the U.S., so you study 5-6 years and graduate with the equivalent of a Master's degree. I remember that by my third year in school I didn't know what I was going to do with a Master's in Literature and Philosophy. I thought: "I don't want to teach, I want to write! I want to be in the publishing industry." It was a very difficult period as I felt I was wasting my time and by the end of so many years in school I would not find a job. So, I began exploring different alternatives. I talked to business professors and to professionals who worked in different areas of marketing and publishing until I found out that, if I took courses in marketing, I would have more options. I could work in the editorial or marketing departments of a publishing house. That is how I ended up doing all those internships I mentioned at the beginning of the book.

Choosing the right major can open lots of doors for the future and it can help you get internships at companies looking for students with your major. Remember when we talked about internships? There are companies such as ExxonMobil interested in students with an engineering major, and others like Dell interested in students with an information technology major, and so on. So, yes, as I said before, declaring your major is very important but you should also feel free to change your major if, after taking a few courses, you realize that is not what you want to do. Students change their majors all the time, just as adults change careers several times during their life.

WORDS OF ENCOURAGEMENT

"Always think positive! Do not ever think that you can't do something. Like my parents always say: the only limitations are the ones you put on yourself. A Zimbabwe proverb says: If you can walk, you can dance. If you can talk, you can sing."

—Jocelyn Acosta, junior at Cornell University

The Right Fit

I spent a lot of time at the beginning of the book, helping you evaluate the different aspects of choosing the right school. Yet, if you are

already in college that section might have come too late in your deci-
sion-making process, right?

But the truth is that it's never too late to change schools if you feel you
are not where you belong. Leylha Ahuile, the founder of Tinta Fresca,
says that: "Too often students want to go to the best school for the career
they wish to pursue. So, if they want to study business they look for the
best business school out there. But you can't just go to the best school for
your career; you have to see what environment will fit you better."

She has first hand experience on the issue. Having started Kinder-
garten when she was 2 years old, Leylha entered college at 16. "Living
in a Chicago suburb, I ended up attending Northern Illinois University
because it was the closest university to my house (1 hour 15 minutes)
where I could still have the 'going away to college' experience. So, I
didn't get to choose the best fit for me. I wanted to go to a smaller
Lutheran college where people from my church went, but my parents
felt it was too far from home. Northern Illinois was the wrong school
for me because it was very large. My parents, both college graduates
from universities in Chile, didn't understand how the system worked
here and neither did I. The environment at a smaller school would have
suited me better."

Going to a school too large for you can contribute to a sense of feeling lost and frustrated. You may feel disconcerted, anonymous and
feel that you have nobody to turn to for guidance. But the size of a
school is by no means the only factor that may feel uncomfortable and
in turn interfere with your ability to succeed. Sometimes, you may have
chosen a college that sounded ideally suited for you, only to find out
later that it wasn't a good choice after all.

Andrea Sáenz from HACE, had an experience along these lines. "I
moved from Southern California to Oregon for school because the

college I chose sounded like my ideal: Small, liberal arts, very rigorous, and academically serious. All this was true and it worked for me. I was, however, very negatively affected by the constant grey and drizzle in Oregon. I was happy with my classes and classmates but unhappy with the environment. I decided to transfer to a small liberal arts college in Southern California and did so for my junior year. It was a great decision. I met new people while keeping in touch with the first group of classmates and I experienced two very different college cultures, both of which had their strengths."

Whatever the reason might be for you to be feeling like you don't belong in the school where you are right now, I suggest that you actively look into it and you take some action. Granted, you may need to be patient during your freshman year as most of your discomfort may stem from the new experience of living away from home, being surrounded by people you don't know and adjusting to college life. But once you realize that the feeling doesn't go away and it interferes with your performance, don't sit around waiting for it to pass. Try to find a college advisor who takes an interest in you and helps you sort things out.

Transferring Schools

As I mentioned in Chapter 5, if you're thinking of transferring to another college, it's a good idea to talk to an adviser to help you figure out the requirements. In Jocelyn's case, the transfer entailed two letters of recommendation, a mid year report, a final transcript, plus, she had to fill out FAFSA and a CSS/Financial Aid Profile® (This is the financial aid application service of the College Board which is used by more than 600 colleges, universities, graduate and professional schools and scholarship programs to determine eligibility for non federal student aid funds). Every college is different, though, so make sure you find out what yours requires.

Given that Jocelyn is a Premed student, she was also required to take Chemistry I over the summer before she transferred. "I had taken Chemistry I during high school and was exempt from taking it at SUNY Buffalo. Once I transferred, my high school credit didn't count even though I had already taken Chemistry 2. I was forced to go backwards," she shares.

Although it's unfortunate that she had to retake a course she had already taken, things like this will happen. But, if you feel like transferring to another school opens a lot more doors for you, these inconveniences will be a small price to pay. Be patient with the process and with adjusting to the new environment, which can take a while.

Jocelyn, for instance, moved from a large state university in Buffalo, the second largest city in New York State, with a population of around 295,000 people and a metropolitan area of around 1,170,000 inhabitants, to an Ivy League School in Ithaca small city of 30,000 people and a metropolitan area of around 100,000. "I love it at Cornell," she says. "At first it was a hard adjustment as I would always compare Cornell with Buffalo. Cornell is more challenging academically and I have grown to appreciate the challenge, it has also made me more openminded. However, I still miss Buffalo greatly and that's the reason it took me longer to open up to people around me in my new school. It was much easier for many transfers at Cornell who are happy to be here since they hated their previous school."

Obviously, it's always easier to start off as a freshman in a school because you form friendships and connections with professors earlier. In a school such as Cornell University, you are also aware from the get go of how challenging your university is. Jocelyn, as many transfer students who are no longer freshmen, faced the challenge of learning to manage her time at her new school while keeping up with her new classes. "It's tough to learn quickly how to manage your time between social and academic life when you are taking more advance courses," she says. Which brings back the point of being patient with yourself and with the process. In addition, finding a support network should be one of your first priorities in your new school.

Steps to Transfer Schools

One of the characteristics of the American higher education system is the ease with which you can transfer from one college to another. Many colleges have special articulation agreements with other institutions, which allow students to transfer from one school to another as part of a program of study with little or no loss of credit and time. Whether it is because you realize the school you initially chose is not a good fit, or because you want to take advantage of a program not offered at your current school, if you wish to transfer, here are the steps you need to follow:

1. First you need to find out if the program to which you wish to transfer, accepts transfer students. At the University of Iowa, for example, only eight of the university's eleven academic colleges admit transfer students.

2. Find out if your school and the one you wish to transfer to are on the same academic calendar. That is, are they on a semester system or a quarter system? Students who successfully complete a course offered in a semester, earn semester credit hours. Colleges require a certain number of semester hours for graduation, so make sure you find out how many you already have and how many you will have to fulfill in the new school.

3. Usually, if you transfer from two-year institution, there is a maximum number of credits you can transfer towards a degree. Some universities don't have a maximum for students who transfer from a four-year institution, so find out what the limit is before transferring.

4. Visit the website of the college to which you wish to transfer to find out the transfer requirements. Some colleges require a certain GPA, and SAT/ACT scores plus an official high school transcript if you transfer with less than certain number of credits.

5. Apply a semester in advance.

6. Apply online; it's faster. Remember to complete your FAFSA in January to ensure aid for the upcoming year.

7. Check for scholarships.

8. If you know alumni from the college to which you wish to transfer, ask them to write a letter of recommendation to the admissions office. It will be a great door opener.

9. Correspond frequently with the college to which you are transferring to make sure everyone is on the same page.

10. Try to visit the campus to which you are transferring and get a sense of the layout of the school. It will make it easier to hit the ground running once you move in.

If you are taking ESL (English as a Second Language) classes in your freshman year, some colleges may not accept these classes for transfer.

WORDS OF ENCOURAGEMENT

*"One of the most important pieces of advice
I can give is to have a support system and not be afraid
of admitting when things get too difficult for you. Approach your
family, friends or faculty when you simply need to talk,
hear advice or just need direction to resolve a situation.
Don't forget that feeling challenged is part of being in college
and there is no reason to feel discouraged and give up!"*

—Paloma I. Veloz, senior student at Syracuse University

CHAPTER RESOURCES

www.collegetransfer.net—Offers lots of information on transferring schools to help you through the process.

www.collegeboard.com—Offers information about transferring schools and choosing a school that would fit your needs.

Books

How to Succeed in College!: Choosing a Major, Transferring and Completing your Degree in Four Years or Less, by Mark Mach (Paperback, 2004).

Transitions: A Guide for the Transfer Student, by Susan B. Weir (Paperback, 2007).

Community Colleges: A Reference Handbook, by David L. Levinson, Danny Weil (Paperback, 2005).

For more information and a constantly updated list of resources log on to **www.latinosincollege.com**.

Chapter 18

PREPARING FOR LIFE AFTER COLLEGE

One of the most important decisions you have to make as you approach graduation is whether you should continue on to grad school now, or you should get a few years of real life experience before you pursue your graduate degree. There are certain careers that require you to take time off from school and enter the workforce to obtain experience. For example, to get an MBA (Master in Business Administration) or a CPA degree (Certified Public Accountant) you need to spend certain number of years working.

Straight to Grad School

Gladys Bernett, the business consultant and owner of Intercontinental Trade, LLC, went straight to graduate school after college: "I was in 'study-mode' so I decided to continue on because it was going to be harder to finish school, start working and then come back in a few years. But also, I couldn't work in hospital administration without a Master's degree. At the same time one of the requirements of that type of job was to have work experience, so I solved the problem by doing a six-month paid internship with a consulting company."

If the career of your choice doesn't require work experience, you then have the option of pursuing your Master's or professional degree right after college or entering the job market. There are advantages and disadvantages to both decisions, but either way you should keep in mind that people with a graduate degree make more money and have a lower rate of unemployment than people with an undergrad degree. So, even if you postpone getting one, a graduate degree is something to aim for.

Education Pays

Here's the median weekly income and level of unemployment by educational attainment.

Education	Weekly Income	Unemployment Rate
High school graduate	$604	4.4%
Some college, no degree	$683	3.8%

Education	Weekly Income	Unemployment Rate
Associate degree	$740	3.0%
Bachelor's degree	$987	2.2%
Master's degree	$1,165	1.8%
Professional degree	$1,427	1.3%
Doctoral degree	$1,497	1.4%

Source: Bureau of Labor Statistics, Current Population Survey, 2007.

Pursuing a Graduate Degree Right After College

Let's look at the pros and cons of getting your graduate degree right after college:

Pros

- You are already in 'school mode.'

- It's easier to focus on your studies while you don't have a family or other commitments, such as a job.

- You're no more likely to have more freedom to relocate to pursue the program you like.

- Having a graduate degree will help you climb the career ladder faster.

Cons

- Some graduate programs require work experience.

- You won't be making money as soon as you would if you were to get a job after college.

- You don't have the opportunity of working in a field for a while to see what graduate degree would be most appropriate or fruitful for you.

You will need to do some thinking to figure out what is the best option for you. I suggest that you talk to your mentors and to people who work in the fields in which you are interested to help you make the right decision.

Finding a Job

I've already talked about the importance of seeking internships while in college. They not only open your eyes regarding the careers that might interest you but they also enable you to make good contacts. In addition, internships frequently lead to job offers upon graduation. I hope you take this advice seriously and pursue several opportunities before you graduate, as they will make a big difference in your career. Having a degree is a fantastic accomplishment but unfortunately, it's no guarantee that you will have a job waiting for you. So, to avoid surprises, you are better off doing your legwork before you finish your studies.

The process of finding a job right after college is the subject of another book altogether. You need to learn how to prepare a resumé, a cover letter, how to interview well, and how to negotiate your first salary, which, in itself, will determine your income possibilities for the rest of your life. Many studies show that women, as a result of not negotiating their first salary after college as often as men do, make less money throughout their careers. This is due to the fact that your salary increases are based on your current salary, so if you begin with a lower salary base, all your increases will consequently be lower.

Two of my previous books: *How to get a job in the U.S., guide for Latinos, and The Latino Advantage in the Workplace*, co-authored with

Arturo Poiré (both published by Sourcebooks), may be useful to you at this point.

You should review the materials included in the Chapter Resources section and you must also consult with your school's career development office to get guidance. They can help you with all aspects of your job search. Schools usually organize job fairs, offer career planning and counseling, online resources, training on interview skills and so on.

Taking Advantage of the Career Center

Paloma I. Veloz, the senior student at Syracuse University, comments on how she got her first internship at a career fair hosted by her school at the end of her sophomore year. Her approach works equally well when you're looking for a job. "I went to my career center several times before the career fair. One of the advisors helped me improve my cover letter and resumé. I interviewed with several companies, but I was able to land an internship with my first choice. I definitely encourage people to take advantage of the career center at their school to research opportunities and prepare for interviews." As a matter of fact, one of the key skills you can practice with your career advisor is interviewing on the phone. "Interviews over the phone aren't as easy as I thought because obviously you're not able to meet with the interviewer fact to face. I tried being very concise with my answers and made sure I let my personality come through as much as possible. I don't recommend over thinking what you're going to say too much, but you have to do your homework. You need to get a good sense of the company you're interviewing with and most importantly, why you want to work for it."

Paloma brings up two very important issues of which you need to be clear before you go on a job interview: 1) You need to know what the company does, what it stands for, where it operates and as much information as you can gather from places like their website, newspaper articles, etc.; and 2) Make sure you know why you want to work for a certain company (for instance, you like their vision, their environmental philosophy, the quality of their product or services, etc.).

Doing research before you send in an application for a job is crucial to your success because you have to customize your resume to the job for which you are applying and you have to be ready to take that screening phone interview (which usually comes before the face to face meeting) and make a good impression. But, as I said, there are plenty of resources listed at the end of this chapter that you need to review before you begin your job quest.

You Have a Degree. Now What?

Rosanna Durruthy, founder of the Aequus Group (www.aequus group.com) and a career development expert, has a few suggestions that you should take seriously.

• Be aware that your career begins when you are in school. The people you meet in your undergraduate life represent important future relationships. They may become references for your work ethic and commitment, offering insights into your good character. These relationships can be valuable in supporting your aspirations and offering proof of your personal integrity.

- **Your college education may provide the skills and knowledge to begin your career but your professional development will require the discipline of continuous learning.** Success is the return on the ongoing investment in learning which comes from a broad range of sources including post graduate studies, membership in professional and affinity organizations, reading industry periodicals, professional certifications and employer sponsored classroom training.

- **Be yourself, because who you are matters.** In time, your career accomplishments will overshadow your GPA. The quality of your work and the quality of your relationships at work will provide the content for the opportunities you seek. Your authenticity as an individual will grow increasingly important with your career progression. Ultimately, trust will be the basis for the hiring decision. We trust the people we know, often because we've seen them interact in different environments, and we believe we know how they will respond under certain circumstances. Over time, the people you work with will view your character as a determinant for the opportunities you seek. When they don't know who you are, they don't see you. They can only see the job you do and so you become the job. Being yourself will allow you to feel more comfortable at work and will help prevent you from becoming invisible to others in your environment.

- **Manage your career.** Your aspirations and objectives can be achieved more readily when you proactively assume responsibility for your career plan and enlist the support of others, rather than waiting for others to notice you. Alone, no one can create success, but in partnership, your success grows stronger when you take the lead in managing your career."

I believe these are wonderful recommendations on which to build your professional career. Come back to them often as you step out into the world of work and find yourself in need of inspiration.

CHAPTER RESOURCES

www.ihispano.com—A search engine and social network specialized in Latino professionals.

www.latpro.com—A search engine specialized in Latino professionals.

www.hace-usa.org—Hispanic Alliance for Career Enhancement. This organization helps recent graduates in the process of finding a job and advancing in their careers. It offers career conferences, mentoring programs, a Latino recruitment series, a high school internship program and many other services.

www.aftercollege.com —This website offers a network for college students and recent grads.

www.collegegrad.com—This website specializes in jobs for recent college graduates. It offers a wide range of advice for your first job after school.

www.iweev.com—A great website to do online job searches, build your professional network and connect with coaches and mentors.

Books

The College Student's Step-by-Step Guide to Landing a Job by Mike Krush (The Samuels Intellectual Capital Group, LLC, 2005).

Do What You Are: Discover the Perfect Career for you Through the Secrets of Personality Type, by Paul D. Tieger (Paperback, 2001).

Getting from College to Career: 90 Things to Do Before You Join the Real World, by Lindsey Pollak (Harper Collins, 2007).

The Complete Job Search Book for College Students: A Step-by-Step Guide to Finding the Right Job, by Richard Walsh and Michelle Soltwedel (F + W Publications Inc., 2007).

Leaving Campus and Going to Work, by T. Jason Smith (Aspen Mountain Publishing, 2006).

How to Survive the Real World: Life After College Graduation: Advice from 774 Graduates Who Did, by Hundreds of Heads and Andrea Syrtash (Hundreds of Heads Books, LLC, 2006).

You Are Too Smart for This: Beating the 100 Lies About Your First Job, by Michael Ball (Sourcebooks, 2006).

Get a Job! Interview Survival Skills for College Students, by John R. Cunningham (Paperback, 2005).

Get the Job! The Fast Guide to Answering Tough Questions on Job Interviews, by David S. Seal (Trafford, 2005).

Best Resumés for College Students and New Grads: Jumpstart Your Career! by Louise M. Kursmark (Paperback, 2005).

For more information and a constantly updated list of resources log on to **www.latinosincollege.com**.

Chapter 19

SEND ME
YOUR STORY!

Your college experience is uniquely yours and it may help others understand certain things better. It may enlighten aspects I didn't touch upon or offer a different perspective on a specific topic. That's why I'd love for you to email me with your own story so I may include quotes from you in future editions. How would you like to see yourself in print?

Here are a few things you could send me:

• A well-written page or two on:

  • A specific experience that you had that relates to any of the chapters in this book. For example, how did having a mentor impact you in college? Or, how did you go about forming your own Latino organization in a campus that lacked one that you liked?

- Overcoming some obstacle that was standing in your way to pursuing a college education.

- Overcoming any type of difficult situation while you were in college.

• Tips on any of the areas covered by the book or on a specific area not covered here but that is relevant to the Latino college experience. For example:

  • More tips on getting scholarships.

  • Tips on things to do and not to do to succeed in school.

  • More tips on good study habits.

  • Ideas to stand out in a large college campus.

  • Ideas to better balance work and study.

  • Tips on good internship opportunities.

  • Tips on great study abroad programs.

  • Names of additional organizations or resources I should list in this book.

  • Great websites that helped you during college.

  • Advice for transfer students.

• A letter telling me what part of this book helped you, what tips you implemented, how it changed your outlook on college, etc.

If you send any materials to be considered for publication in future editions of this book, you are accepting that I have the right to publish them in whole or in part. I will email you a form that further explains what you are agreeing to.

Email your contributions to:

mariela@latinosincollege.com

Visit my blog at: http://marielablog.com

And my website: www.marieladbbah.com

A FEW FINALS WORDS

As you arrive to the end of this book, I hope you found some useful advice, some Words of Encouragement to brighten your years in school, and some good resources to further explore the different topics I touched upon.

You are in the middle of one of the most incredible times of your life and it is my hope that you live every day as if it were your last; that you rise to the challenges in front of you; that you never doubt your abilities, gifts and talents; that you always give your best and work hard and that you avoid limiting yourself in any way.

But most of all, I wish that you dream big because the truth is, that the sky is not the limit. You are. You set your own expectations and limitations and you believe in them. You decide whether you are capable of achieving grandness or not. You decide if you are going to make a difference in this world or not. So make sure you set your expectations as high as your imagination will take you.

Here's to your success! Cheers!

RESOURCES

Appendix 1

List of Top Colleges for Latino Students

This list is compiled by *Hispanic Outlook Magazine* and it reflects the colleges that in 2006/2007 are enrolling and graduating the largest number of Latino students

Colleges awarding the most bachelors degrees to Hispanics, 2006*

Rank	Institution Name	State	Total
1	FLORIDA INTERNATIONAL UNIVERSITY	FL	3169
2	THE UNIVERSITY OF TEXAS-PAN AMERICAN	TX	2148
3	THE UNIVERSITY OF TEXAS AT EL PASO	TX	1839
4	THE UNIVERSITY OF TEXAS AT SAN ANTONIO	TX	1786
5	CALIFORNIA STATE UNIVERSITY-FULLERTON	CA	1505
6	SAN DIEGO STATE UNIVERSITY	CA	1399
7	CALIFORNIA STATE UNIVERSITY-LONG BEACH	CA	1392
8	CALIFORNIA STATE UNIVERSITY-NORTHRIDGE	CA	1360
9	CALIFORNIA STATE UNIVERSITY-LOS ANGELES	CA	1308
10	THE UNIVERSITY OF TEXAS AT AUSTIN	TX	
11	UNIVERSITY OF FLORIDA	FL	
12	UNIVERSITY OF CALIFORNIA-LOS ANGELES CA	1	

13	UNIVERSITY OF CENTRAL FLORIDA	FL	1058
14	UNIVERSITY OF HOUSTON	TX	1003
15	UNIVERSITY OF NEW MEXICO-MAIN CAMPUS	NM	968
16	TEXAS STATE UNIVERSITY-SAN MARCOS	TX	920
17	CALIFORNIA STATE POLYTECHNIC UNIVERSITY-POMONA	CA	888
18	NEW MEXICO STATE UNIVERSITY-MAIN CAMPUS	NM	874
19	THE UNIVERSITY OF TEXAS AT BROWNSVILLE	TX	831
20	ARIZONA STATE UNIVERSITY AT THE TEMPE CAMPUS	AZ	819
21	CALIFORNIA STATE UNIVERSITY-SAN BERNARDINO	CA	818
22	UNIVERSITY OF ARIZONA	AZ	817
23	CALIFORNIA STATE UNIVERSITY-FRESNO	CA	794
24	TEXAS A & M UNIVERSITY	TX	769
25	UNIVERSITY OF CALIFORNIA-SANTA BARBARA	CA	752
26	UNIVERSITY OF CALIFORNIA-RIVERSIDE	CA	744
27	UNIVERSITY OF PHOENIX-ONLINE CAMPUS	AZ	744
28	FLORIDA ATLANTIC UNIVERSITY	FL	738
29	FLORIDA STATE UNIVERSITY	FL	733
30	TEXAS A & M UNIVERSITY-KINGSVILLE	TX	691
31	UNIVERSITY OF SOUTH FLORIDA	FL	684
32	CALIFORNIA STATE UNIVERSITY-DOMINGUEZ HILLS	CA	647
33	UNIVERSITY OF HOUSTON-DOWNTOWN	TX	644
34	SAN FRANCISCO STATE UNIVERSITY	CA	643
35	CALIFORNIA STATE UNIVERSITY-SACRAMENTO	CA	641
36	TEXAS A & M INTERNATIONAL UNIVERSITY	TX	641
37	UNIVERSITY OF CALIFORNIA-BERKELEY	CA	639
38	UNIVERSITY OF MIAMI	FL	620
39	SAN JOSE STATE UNIVERSITY	CA	604
40	UNIVERSITY OF CALIFORNIA-DAVIS	CA	584
41	UNIVERSITY OF SOUTHERN CALIFORNIA	CA	558
42	UNIVERSITY OF CALIFORNIA-IRVINE	CA	551
43	CUNY LEHMAN COLLEGE	NY	548
	THE UNIVERSITY OF TEXAS AT ARLINGTON	TX	536

45	CUNY JOHN JAY COLLEGE CRIMINAL JUSTICE	NY	535
46	UNIVERSITY OF NORTH TEXAS	TX	523
47	UNIVERSITY OF CALIFORNIA-SAN DIEGO	CA	513
48	TEXAS TECH UNIVERSITY	TX	502
49	UNIVERSITY OF CALIFORNIA-SANTA CRUZ	CA	460
50	BARRY UNIVERSITY	FL	453
51	CALIFORNIA STATE UNIVERSITY-BAKERSFIELD	CA	438
52	UNIVERSITY OF ILLINOIS AT CHICAGO	IL	436
53	RUTGERS UNIVERSITY-NEW BRUNSWICK	NJ	432
54	TEXAS A & M UNIVERSITY-CORPUS CHRISTI	TX	427
55	PARK UNIVERSITY	MO	408
56	UNIVERSITY OF ILLINOIS AT URBANA-CHAMPAIGN	IL	407
57	UNIVERSITY OF LA VERNE	CA	389
58	CUNY HUNTER COLLEGE	NY	388
59	UNIVERSITY OF THE INCARNATE WORD	TX	378
60	NEW YORK UNIVERSITY	NY	376
61	MONTCLAIR STATE UNIVERSITY	NJ	370
62	CUNY BERNARD M BARUCH COLLEGE	NY	364
63	DEPAUL UNIVERSITY	IL	360
64	CUNY CITY COLLEGE	NY	354
65	NORTHERN ARIZONA UNIVERSITY	AZ	348
66	NOVA SOUTHEASTERN UNIVERSITY	FL	348
67	UNIVERSITY OF NEVADA-LAS VEGAS	NV	340
68	CALIFORNIA STATE UNIVERSITY-STANISLAUS	CA	339
69	ST JOHN'S UNIVERSITY-NEW YORK	NY	339
70	KEAN UNIVERSITY	NJ	332
71	UNIVERSITY OF COLORADO AT BOULDER	CO	326
72	UNIVERSITY OF MARYLAND-COLLEGE PARK	MD	321
73	ST MARYS UNIVERSITY	TX	
74	CUNY QUEENS COLLEGE	NY	
75	CALIFORNIA POLYTECHNIC STATE UNIVERSITY-SAN LUIS OBISPO	CA	

76	PENNSYLVANIA STATE UNIVERSITY-MAIN CAMPUS	PA	305
77	MERCY COLLEGE-MAIN CAMPUS	NY	296
78	GEORGE MASON UNIVERSITY	VA	296
79	NEW JERSEY CITY UNIVERSITY	NJ	287
80	DEVRY UNIVERSITY-CALIFORNIA	CA	286
81	CALIFORNIA STATE UNIVERSITY-EAST BAY	CA	285
82	MONROE COLLEGE-MAIN CAMPUS	NY	283
83	UNIVERSITY OF WASHINGTON-SEATTLE CAMPUS	WA	280
84	CALIFORNIA STATE UNIVERSITY-SAN MARCOS	CA	280
85	NORTHEASTERN ILLINOIS UNIVERSITY	IL	278
86	METROPOLITAN STATE COLLEGE OF DENVER	CO	270
87	STONY BROOK UNIVERSITY	NY	266
88	ARIZONA STATE UNIVERSITY AT THE WEST CAMPUS	AZ	259
89	OUR LADY OF THE LAKE UNIVERSITY-SAN ANTONIO	TX	252
90	DEVRY UNIVERSITY-ILLINOIS	IL	248
91	CALIFORNIA STATE UNIVERSITY-CHICO	CA	246
92	SAM HOUSTON STATE UNIVERSITY	TX	242
93	LOYOLA MARYMOUNT UNIVERSITY	CA	239
94	UNIVERSITY OF MICHIGAN-ANN ARBOR	MI	231
95	BRIGHAM YOUNG UNIVERSITY	UT	231
96	EMBRY RIDDLE AERONAUTICAL UNIVERSITY-WORLDWIDE	FL	228
97	SAINT EDWARD'S UNIVERSITY	TX	225
98	ROBERT MORRIS COLLEGE	IL	221
99	NORTHERN ILLINOIS UNIVERSITY	IL	217
100	MICHIGAN STATE UNIVERSITY	MI	216

* Reprinted with permission of *Hispanic Outlook Magazine*. Visit their website at www.hispanicoutlook.com for more information and articles on Hispanics in Higher Education.

Appendix 2

List of Websites that List or Offer Scholarships for Latinos

www.chci.org/chciyouth/scholarship/scholarship.htm—The Congressional Hispanic Caucus Institute awards scholarships to Latino students who have a history of performing public service-oriented activities in their communities and who plan to continue contributing in the future.

www.hacu.net—Directory of scholarships.

www.hispanicfund.org—Offers a variety of scholarships sponsored by various corporations.

www.hsf.net—Offers a variety of scholarships sponsored by various corporations.

www.latinocollegedollars.org—Directory of scholarships compiled by the Tomas Rivera Policy Institute.

www.meencanta.com—Ronald McDonald House Charities/HACER scholarship website.

www.scholarshipsforhispanics.com—Directory of Scholarships.

http://scholarships.fatomei.com/hispanics.html—A comprehensive directory of scholarships listed by organization and type of program. Covers scholarships for K-Postgraduate studies.

Appendix 3

List of Key Professional Latino Associations

www.aaha.org—Association of Hispanic Advertising Agencies

www.alpfa.org—The Association of Latino Professionals in Finance and Accounting

www.a-lista.org—Latinos on Information, Science and Technology Association

www.hacr.org—Hispanic Association on Corporate Responsibility

www.hispanichr.org—Society of Hispanic Human Resource Executives

www.hnba.com—Hispanic National Bar Association

www.lswo.org —Latino Social Workers Organization

www.nabe.org—National Association for Bilingual Education

www.nhba.org—National Hispanic Business Association

www.nahj.org—National Association of Hispanic Journalists

www.nhmamd.org—National Hispanic Medical Association

www.nahp.org—National Association of Hispanic Publications

www.nshmba.org—National Society of Hispanic MBAs

www.nshp.org—National Society of Hispanic Professionals

www.shpe.org—Society of Hispanic Professional Engineers

www.thehispanicnurses.org—National Association of Hispanic Nurses

Appendix 4

List of Best Companies for Diverse Talent

The following is a list of companies that consistently get picked by various list-compilation organizations as some of the best for diverse talent. I placed a star next to those companies that often get mentioned as particularly good for Latinos.

Abbott

Accenture

Aetna

Allstate Insurance Company

American Express *

AT&T*

Avon Products

Bank of America *

Blue Cross and Blue Shield of Florida*

Bright Horizons Family Solutions

Capital One Financial Corp.

Citigroup *

Colgate Palmolive

Cox Communications

CSX

Cummins

Daren Restaurants*

Deloitte LLP

Denny's Spartanburg, S.C.

Eastman Kodak

Ernst & Young

Fannie Mae Washington DC

Ford Motor Co.

General Mills

General Motors

Health Care Service Corp.

Henry Ford Health System

Hilton Hotels Corp.

HSBC Bank USA, NA*

IBM*

Johnson & Johnson

JPMorgan Chase

Kaiser Permanente*

KeyBank

KPMG

Kraft Foods

Macy's

Marriott International*

MasterCard Worldwide

McDonald's Corporation*

Merck & Co.

Merrill Lynch & Co.

Monsanto Co.

New York Life Insurance*

Nordstrom

Novartis Pharmaceuticals Corp.

Pepsi Bottling Group*

PepsiCo

PG &E Corp.

PricewaterhouseCoopers

Procter & Gamble*

Prudential Financial*

Sempra Energy

Schering-Plough

Sodexho*

Shouthern California Edison

Sprint

Starwood Hotels & Resorts Worldwide

State Farm Mutual Insurance Companies

The Coca-Cola Co.

The Walt Disney Co.*

Toyota Motor North America

Turner Broadcasting System

Union Bank of California

United Parcel Service

Verizon Communications*

Wachovia*

Washington Mutual

WellPoint

Wells Fargo & Co.*

Kerox Corp.

Yum Brands Louisville

Appendix 5

Additional Books About College

Confessions of a College Freshman: A Survival Guide for Dorm Life, Biology Lab, the Cafeteria, and Other First-Year Adventures by Zach Arrington.

Entrar en la Universidad: Una Guía para el Estudiante Hispano, by K.Patricia Aviezer.

Everything you Ever Wanted to Know About College: A Guide for Minority Students, by Dr. Boyce Watkins.

The Everything College Survival Book: From Social Life to Study Skills—All you need to know to fit right in! by Michael S. Malone.

The Real Freshman Handbook: A Totally Honest Guide to Life on Campus by Jennifer Hanson.

What Teens Need to Succeed: Proven, Practical Ways to Shape your Own Future, by Peter L.Benson, Ph.D., Judy Galbraith, M.A. and Pamela Espeland.

Winning Scholarships for College, an Insider's Guide, by Marianne Ragins (winner of more than $400,000 in scholarship money).

Picture Gallery

Using the resources in this book,
you can be a scholarship winner and get great internships!

2008 Winners of the RMHC/HACER New York
(tri-state area) Scholarship
www.meencanta.com

Samuel Cruz and Brian Campos, 2008 winners of two of the four
$100,000 RMHC/HACER national scholarships with Roberto Madan,
a McDonald's owner/operator and one of
the scholarship's most fervent supporters
www.meencanta.com

Hispanic Scholarship Fund' scholarship recipients at their
"Celebration of Achievement" event, Miami, 2007
www.hsf.net

A recent group of interns that INROADS placed at UTC, Liberty Mutual, Deloitte, PWC, and MetLife companies. www.INROADS.org

THE AUTHOR

Photo: María Fernanda Hubeaut

Mariela Dabbah founder and champion of the initiative "Latinos in College: Preparing Emerging Leaders for the Workforce," is the award-winning, best-selling author of several titles that help Latinos successfully navigate the American system. She immigrated to the United States from Argentina with two suitcases full of dreams. The beginning was hard: long working hours and little fun. She learned as much as she could from mentors and colleagues and with much hard work, she was eventually able to pursue her writing career. A few years later, she began publishing her books, became a sought after speaker and has appeared as a guest expert on all major Spanish and English media outlets such as ABC's *Good Morning America*, NBC's *Today in New York*, Univision's *Despierta América*, and Yahoo/MSN Latino among many others. You can learn more about her and the Latinos in College campaign at www.latinosincollege.com and on her website: www.marieladabbah.com